Eleven

Self Empowerment

Protocols

R. Neville Johnston

It is time for us to be consistently powerful, from within ourselves.

AuthorHouse™
1663 Liberty Drive, Suite 200
Bloomington, IN 47403
www.authorhouse.com
Phone: 1-800-839-8640

First published by AuthorHouse 3/5/2010
ISBN: 978-1-4490-6221-7 (e)
ISBN: 978-1-4490-6219-4 (sc)
ISBN: 978-1-4490-6220-0 (hc)

Printed in the United States of America
Bloomington, Indiana
This book is printed on acid-free paper.

Library of Congress Control Number: 2009913623

Contents

Dedication

Mary Phelan, your inspiration and everything you have contributed to this volume is infinitely appreciated. Grace and Caramai, what a wise choice for being my beautiful, talented and patient daughters. Ariane, your nobility and recognition are celebratory.

Introduction

A fundamental principle of light and love is always freedom. It is a given. Freedom equals consciousness. As we ascend into the newer age, the more we can recognize ourselves as the active agent behind everything that happens. Therefore we can see that we are sovereign of our life. We are <u>free</u> to create.

In the distant past religion did a very good job of separating us from our power. If the priest said it was so it was so. We had no say in the so. The confessional reduced us to guilty little children seeking forgiveness as though it was something external. Our life was something out of our hands.

The next god was science. The polygraph became the new Monsignor confessor, still with that same effect or reducing us to guilty children. If the new priest, a scientist or a doctor said, it was so, it was so. With the idea that reality is a "fixed" concept, again our life was something that was out of our hands.

Still we live in an age where we are taught that our power is outside of ourselves. This is a falsehood taught by slaves to slaves. Powerlessness is the result of a life of guilt and fear. This concept is just beginning to fade. Lets get on it. Decide right now to correct this glitch in life.

The newer age we are entering is more than a consciousness shift, it is a dimensional shift, and it is a fundamental shift. Everyday more of this new awareness downloads. Watch for it. Participate in it. Own it. The examples are countless.

In our life, every "negative" event transmutes much more rapidly. Almost immediately we recognize any such situation as a faculty by which we create an increasingly compassionate outlook. It doesn't take years anymore. Our concepts of time and the timeline have shifted. Sales of metaphysical books and CDs have sky rocketed. We are well on our way to ascension.

A very important part of this newness is that each of us came with an incarnational contract. This agreement outlines the evolutionary advance we will make in this lifetime. It's nice to know we have such a document guiding us. One is given to wonder what specifics are included. What does your evolutionary contract say? What lessons did you come here to master?

Very few of us ever get to the bottom line in this contract. For all of us this last line states that we will become whole. This is to say, complete within ourselves as well as being members of our family, our community and our planet, even our galaxy.

As we achieve this wholeness, we begin to seek others, who are whole, in order to form different sorts of relationships. A relationship between two people, who are whole results in "greater than the sum of the parts." Currently the co-dependent relationships result in less than the sum of the parts because, when we enable others, we cut them off from their feedback, their growth and their independence.

This book is designed to assist each of us to be our own best counselor, our own best friend and our own best practitioner. As we re-train ourselves to find all the answers within our selves, and they are all there, we will become masters of our own growth. This is not to discount the wisdom passed down form others and elders. This is not to keep us from seeking counsel. This is to add to it. The way it is, self-correction is a right that is taken away from us before we knew we had it. Here in lies the restoration. It's no longer about the experience, it is about you.

Protocol One

I Claim My Power

> *"Although the world is full of suffering,*
> *It is also full of overcoming it."*
>
> Helen Keller

Tomorrow, observe the hypnagogic state we're in, after we have become aware that we are awake and before we make the decision to open our eyes. It's one of the most powerful states of mind in our entire cycle. Colossal reprogramming can occur at this time.

Normally this doorway is used poorly because whatever it is that we did yesterday, that which we disapprove of, comes flooding into our thoughts and we begin our day in a deficit.

More commonly an alarm clock shatters us into consciousness and one hundred percent of this opportunity is voided. The first thought becomes, "I <u>have</u> to get up." "Have to" is a bully speaking and this does not serve us as a way to begin something so sacred as a day.

Retrain yourself to repeat, "I claim my power," before you open your eyes. This will create a very different day. As you get use to relaxing in this hypnagogic state other things can be added. At this point, one foot is in the dream world and the other is in reality.

From this position we can make decisions about our reality and visit realms of creation unfamiliar to the awake mind. As we become better and better at mastering this hypnagogic consciousness, ask to see below from above. Then ask specifically how above affects below and vice versa.

(2)

Many years ago one could ask someone, "What percent of your reality do you create?" And hear answers like seventeen percent. One would wonder who was creating the other eighty three percent. As the decades flew by the new question became: "All right, you create one hundred percent of your reality. Now what percent of the time do you realize this?" This time we would be hearing answers like, "I remember that I create all of my reality point zero one seven percent of the time."

The newer question has become: "Why would I create such a reality?" There are many true answers: To evolve, because of the programming, to become less judgmental, and lest we forget the famous yet powerless concept of habit. Whatever it is we are creating we are doing so because it is our lesson. What we can call upon is the idea that our attitude is something we create as well.

These life's experiences are easier thought of as tests, initiations or benchmarks in our ascension. When viewed as such we can recognize their repetition as an asterisk, a bookmark, a glitch in the matrix. Repeated events represent a place where we can approach the pattern, in a new way. In doing so we can pass these points. Instantaneously we gain a different perspective. Now it becomes, "Why am I creating this attitude?" Not why does this always happen to moi?

Any life experience we create can be considered symptomatic of a far greater dynamic. Regardless of how "horrible" an event seems underneath this event the seeds of compassion have been planted.

No matter what happens we have become a better person and that event is to be considered a blessing. A blessing upon analysis, yes, still it was always a blessing, even from the beginning. It's just changing our search engine to recognize, the blessing part, far more readily.

(3)

A final caveat in our study of our own power… In the section on trinities we discuss the concept of power being a form of love, true power that is. In this hypnagogic state, in meditation with the higher self one may find so pure a version of the soul that it responds only lovingly without any judgment as to the circumstance. This is a powerful stance, this is God per se. Were we to respond only lovingly, we would be the most powerful person in the world.

Lets look at the point of taking the Earth ride as the opportunity to develop a tool called discernment. Just owing to the practical limitations of the corporal being, we will not be responding to every situation presented to us on a daily basis. Ergo, we must develop another aspect of love called choice AKA discernment.

As the Toltec say, choose your battles. So life becomes a balance between compassion and discernment. And so this defines the very nature of wisdom. To add up this balance, we would consider service to self (self love) as providing fifty one percent of the formula, and service to others as the other forty nine percent. It is readily visible that, in order to be of service to life one must ensure one's ability to be alive. Again start each day with "I claim my power!"

Protocol Affirmation: I delight to adjust my flight.

Raven Landing

Protocol Two

A First Step Out of The Box

There is a reason that this is not called "<u>The</u> First Step Out of

The Box." This is because the escape from the box involves being free. As long as there is only one correct answer, <u>The Answer</u>, we are bound to it, bound by it. It's not so much bound to the answer, more to the "having the answer." What happens once we "have the answer," is we give up the search for other answers. The search, the breaking through that is our creativity, stops.

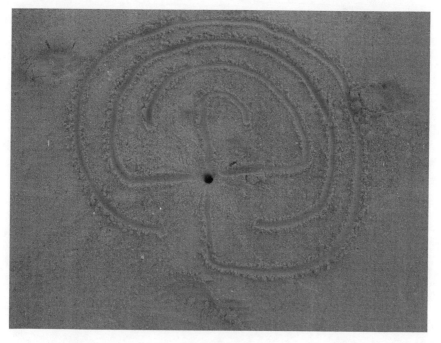

Crablinth

"There is Always More Than One Correct Answer."

As counter intuitive as this sounds it remains true. Our universe is unlimited. It is simply fact. The answer to "What is two plus two?" Is four yes, and it is also nine minus five, ten minus six, etc. Observe that there are an infinite number of correct answers to two plus two. Where someone teaching numerology then twenty-two is an answer that serves well. In balancing a checkbook, four is an answer that is more fitting.

Each and every one of us has a different opinion. The thing is that an individual's opinion is correct for them at that time. Any person is at the height of their evolutionary potential at all times, even though this varies minute to minute and only rarely appears so.

At the point that, our own thinking no longer holds us in one place, "one correct answer," we begin to be free. Within this growth our very language changes. One can now say things like, " another aspect of this is... A different facet of this reveals... In my opinion, etc."

Any number of teachers have advocated some method by which we entitle ourselves to have both sides of our brain turned on at the same time. With practice we can have them both turned all the time.

These exercises can be as simple as listening to the note C and the note B being played at the same time. These notes hold the activator codes for the lobes.

In the primitive past, a composer could be excommunicated for writing music where C and B played simultaneously. It was called "The Devil's note." Its sound turns on the brain. And the church would not sanction anything that would wake up the flock.

For those of us that prefer a tactile approach to turning on the whole brain, touch each earlobe or shoulder or side of the body with the opposite hand. In other words, grasp the left earlobe with the right hand and vice versa. Then just "be" for a moment.

The visual instrument is to point both index fingers at each other, right in front of you. Cross your eyes until you can a piece of index finger with a nail on both end floating between your two pointer fingers. When you see this phenomenon, it means the brain is receiving information from both eyes at the same time. The result is that both haves switch on.

It is at this point that our brain begins the process of having three separate perceptions. The left-brain formatting is the male, the traditional and acceptable, logical thinking system. The right brain, the more recently popularized approach, is the female, intuitive, feeling process of thought.

Both combine into a third technique. This is the newer still. This last one is only rarely envisioned, until we practice. Then it becomes the modern, the new, the go to thought sanctum. Finally thinking with the whole brain becomes normal. Then our younglings will do it just because it is the environment they live in.

When these new mindsets begin to write enough code our life changes. We become less attached to outcome and more of an explorer of diversity. This is a novel reality, for most of us. Working with a newness, how exciting. Our skill as a diplomat increases exponentially.

This results in a soul level relaxation. Peace comes to us and we no longer have to bang that "war drum" every time anything happens that is unexpected. Say, out loud right now, "I choose to take my next step out of the box!"

Protocol Affirmation: I reprogram to remember who I really am.

Protocol Three
Trinity Thought
Trinities: The Principle of Ascension

The planet we live on, like most planets, has two poles. Which means we live on a bipolar planet. At this point we are a bipolar race. When we say someone has "bipolar disorder," all we are really saying is that they take their time about it. They divide mood swing into days instead of moments like the rest of us. If this is Tuesday I must be depressed.

The movement forward, is progressing into trinity thinking. The observation that the universe runs on two poles is one correct answer. Things seem to be paired in opposites because it is all translated through a polar consciousness.

The rule of trinity is that: Any two things that you think of as opposite indicate that there is a third concept that allows you to see the two things as the same thing.

Red and green, are both color. They are both signals. They are both Christmas, and with out a doubt they are an unorthodox selection of socks. When you triangulate a car battery, the engine comes to life. And so with the human mind, it comes to life when we begin to think in trinities instead of poles. The thought process comes to life.

How's this for an ongoing mystery? Light and darkness occupy the same space at the same time. There were an ancient people who worshiped darkness because it is eternal. In this system of thought a light is seen as temporary, darkness as always there. This concept allows us to see our world in a whole new light.

The *Urantia Book*, is a delightful read. It is 2097 pages long. It took a full lunar cycle (28 days) to read it. Actually it took 23 days to read 2095 pages and five days to finish those last few pages. This was owing to the enormous amount of information and subsequent reformatting involved. This book introduces trinities.

The first paragraph on page 2095:

"There are just three elements in universal reality: fact, idea and relationship. The religious consciousness identifies these realities as science, philosophy, and truth. Philosophy would be inclined to view these activities as reason, wisdom, and faith—physical reality, intellectual reality, and spiritual reality. We are in the habit of designating these realities as thing meaning, and value."

In our language: thesis, antithesis and synthesis. It explains it all, well… All as far as third dimension is concerned.

This conversion from polar thinking to trinity thinking is the device of ascension for the human race. This desire for change, this perpetual curiosity, this constant seeking of enlightenment is all made real in the conversion to thinking in three dynamics instead of two.

One is well advised to convert all the polarity in one's vocabulary. Just to get us started lets chew on a big nugget, the seemingly opposite concepts of good and evil.

Good and evil are the same because: They form a whole. They work together to awaken us. They are pre-judgments. (This is to say they are decided and then observed.) Either one constitutes decision. The two are teams we play for. We have spent lifetimes behind one of them or the other. Both move us. They are a pair, equals, just like yin and yang.

A greater clarity may occur when they are seen as <u>teachers</u>. The darkest deeds ever done have resulted in, getting it quickly, this is to say the great advances. It's the same with good.

Red Rocks

Some Common Trinities:

Body, Mind and Spirit

Perhaps the most widely publicized trinity, the physical mental and spiritual work together in our progression. Our first annotation is that the three each have their own vote. This electoral process determines our evolutionary positioning. In all trinities the principle is revealed by the concept that two third majority rules.

The spirit is always turning in a very high frequency vote. It's its nature. The mind is always the swing vote. And the body turns in a higher frequency vote as the food it consumes and its movement reaches lighter and lighter density. We humans have long fasted and used disciplines like yoga to reach a spiritual enlightenment.

As this trinity rises up, so does the reality that we live. Choice has always been the activator code for free will. Better choices are inevitable. An easy boost is simply the decision to get all three of our elements aligned and on board.

Trinity of the Victim

This is a very common trinity. Humanity as a group, is tangled within it. Many of us speak with that sour note of the victim. This causes the rest of us to do anything to get rid of this noise of powerlessness, as well as the person who is self-indulging in it. In order to out grow the whining paradigm we will first understand it.

The Words Victim and Guilt are Synonymous

The trinity goes: In order to be a victim one must first create a persecutor. Then, even more cleverly, this victim creates a rescuer. The rescuer is more intimately pronounced re-skewer. As we are skewer by the guilt of having been rescued. We "owe" them and therefore are cast into a minion role with them. And so this trinity goes round and round. Persecutor, Victim, Re-skewer or is it: pursuer, victim, and hero?

When we play <u>any one</u> of these three roles we are in the trinity of the victim. We are not saying not to assist. When we are evolved to the point of not becoming mired in other people's drama, then it is possible to gently, as though dealing with a child, untangle someone from their programming. "What will you be doing about this?"

There is no such thing as a victim. Either we have free will, meaning we choose our life, or other people, or some god, or "reality" creates us. Everything in our life occurs with our signature on it. Everything is by our choice. If I am hurt it is because I chose it. I am the <u>only</u> one who can hurt me, even though someone else may pretend to look like they are doing it.

Some Not So Common Trinities:

A Trinity of Three Angels
Clarity, Knowing and Faith

Somewhere in adolescence I read a Sci-Fi story about a tigeress who had forgotten herself and fallen off a mountain ledge to her death. An angel was dispatched and to my surprise this angel caressed the tigeress back to life saying, "<u>Where</u> is your knowing?" This tigeress had two cubs to be raised. "Where is your knowing?"

Years later I found my self calling this angel, calling Clarity. I called on walks. I called in meditation. I wrote affirmations and most of all I decided that I would have Clarity, with a capitol "C." It happened. An angelic came to me and began the trinity that is about to be unfolded for your benefit and of our entire world.

In working with the Angel of Clarity, I found that I could see beyond the appearance of things, things that had been ensconced in the veil of confusion. Clarity in fact means clear as in, "see right through." For some time we played together and eventually she introduced me to her sister. This second angelic is named "Knowing."

Knowing, is to know rather than doubt. It is enormously powerful. It is freedom. A funny expression is, "I thought so." It's not true. What the person is actually saying is, "I didn't believe it." Working with Knowing brought a greater consciousness than I'd ever had.

Soon Clarity and Knowing assisted me to polish up, to the point that the third sister joined us. Her name is Faith. By the way Faiths nickname is Trust. With the trinity complete I began to understand reality from a very different point of view.

Over time Faith explained that: The distance between the event and the recognition of the event as a blessing, that distance is mandated by the amount of fear, doubt, worry and guilt in one's system. When we are free of these anti-vitality concepts; everything becomes immediately recognizable as an on-going blessing. The word for this way of thinking is having faith or trust. Trust that everything always works out in everyone's favor.

Where one thinking that something didn't work out as a blessing? Then we know it happened recently.

Working with this trinity will actually make one more intelligent. Any Mensa book will have someone's definition of intelligence. A few books and one will be deciding their personal definition of intelligence. The first one I thought of was, "Intelligence is the ability to recognize and seize opportunity." How's that for a cognitive index?

Many years of working in this trinity and the definition has rewritten itself. Intelligence is, "The distance between the stimulus and the response." I'm not talking about reaction time. This distance is in words. Intelligence is how we think of the situation.

The less efficient the words we think in the longer it takes to respond. Therefore the more efficiently we think the more intelligent we are. As a service to oneself call this trinity into your life.

Trinity of Human Power

"Love is all there is."

John Lennon (paraphrase)

Love, Imagination and Decision

The first of this trinity is the ability to love. Usually society waits until adolescence to amend this one. It is replaced by judgment (pre-judgment) and then we begin the life long battle between head and heart. Other than this we are born love generators. As a group we are catching on to the idea, that, until everything looks like love and is loveable, we are not yet seeing the true reality. This is simply because love is the only thing there is.

The decommissioning of our love generator causes the eclipse to the all-important self-esteem. Once there is a lack of an inherent self worth, we are easily manipulated by guilt and anyone that tells us we will be a better person if we have an SUV or a bigger house. This is absurd. Each of us is an indispensable note in the symphony that is humanity. Self worth is a birth rite.

We are all love generators. When we love something or someone there is more love than there was before. We generate love. To demo this, think of something cute, that bird that looks just like a chipmunk or a fuzzy bunny. Voila there is more love in the world than there was before and you created it. Go on think of something else that's cute. Whatever you think of as cute, it's something you love, now there is more love. Fun eh?

Love Potato

Imagination

The second part of our trinity is the imagination. It is more powerful than anything. It can over write memory. If you go over an event enough times you can change it in memory. You will remember things that didn't happen. You will forget things that did happen.

The imagination is so powerful we can imagine that we don't love someone. It is the most powerful thing. It is even more powerful than God. People can imagine that God doesn't exist.

In our society, one is not allowed to be this powerful, and so a failsafe a code is written into each of us: "It's just your Imagination." Wham, defeats it instantly. It's an easy enough code to correct, just fire that disenfranchising little voice. At his point, "It's just your imagination," may be very subtle, almost inaudible. It's important to be able to hear it first and then say, "No, it's not…and never say that again." We all have a right to know we are sane.

Lets go forward in our definition of the trinity of human power. We take this love, which we have generated and mold it with the imagination, exactly the way an artist sculpts in terra cotta. Love and imagination, these two are the great faculty of humanity.

The third element is the place where the creation is made manifest, brought into third dimension. This is where we fire the terra cotta just like the artist's sculpture. This is when we <u>decide</u>. The universe itself then automatically brings it into existence. A moment later we could change our minds and it would cease to exist. In our timeline, nothing is more than a decision away.

The Stream of Decisions

We don't necessarily believe that a decision that we make "counts." It does. The fact that we live in a stream of decisions is sometimes invisible to us. Practice until you can trace your thought stream back to the instant that you decided that things would turn out the way they did. It may have been when we were fatigued. Possibly it was due to a belief in self-worthlessness.

A decision will manifest unless there is a subconscious program preventing it from joining us. To do away with this is to suggest that our planet like our mind is divided into two hemispheres. Another way to say it is that the head and heart both have a vote. Both have a correct answer.

The combination of the two answers results in the triangulation of these apparently opposing philosophies. The triangulation results in the command. And the decision puts it in place. The door of manifestation then opens.

The way to check any trinity is to see if it is alive. Does it continue in its movement? The decision results in more love and thus the love results in more imagination and the imagination results in another decision. Yes, it is alive!

The Trinity of Decision

Bless it if it does; bless it if it doesn't, Now Decide.

The Eastern hemisphere, and accurately so, would have us notice that everything is automatically provided for us, thus allowing us to allow, and putting us in a position to just receive. Just be. A correct answer.

In the West, we would suggest going out there and making it happen. Drink fifty cups of coffee, drive a Mustang to work and exercise our free will until it can pump iron with the best of them. Just do. Again this is a correct answer.

It is the merging of these two attributes that conveys us across the finish line. So the technique is to decide that, if things don't go the way you wish…bless it. This means to take the time to look at the future were things do go "amiss." And recognize its perfection. Equally recognize the perfection in having it go the other way, the way "preferred."

Now say bless it if it does; bless it if it doesn't and then decide. This takes the factor of "Attachment to Out Come," away from the process. This makes the decision, the manifestation possible. As long as we are attached to outcome we resist all other outcomes and things freeze up.

Resistance is an unseen use of free will.

Effortlessness is defined as a total absence of resistance. Allowing is our power. When we decide something, the universe engineers it and manifests it. Once the decision is made manifest, it becomes love and this time the imagination played a different role so the trinity continues its cycles. Powerful aren't we? Yes we are!

The Creation Trinity

Flash, Process, Boredom

The flash is our flash of intuition or inspiration. Little known to us is the idea that the intuition is the result of a decision. Decision precedes all. I decide to be and therefore I am.

This inspiration is as a result of stimulation in either the mental or spiritual subconscious. This percolation of an unconscious mind is what triggers the decision and then the inspiration. Look a bird, I decide to fly, therefore the inspiration that became airplane.

Process

The movement of molecules characterizes the second chapter in our trinity, the process. As a small child plays they are in the process of joy. When we appoint our inner child as CEO of our guides, we become always in the state of, always in anticipation of, joy. Without this recognition of joy this part of our trinity may be misconstrued as the "work."

We live in an automatic universe. It's to be noted that only the universe itself does the actual accomplishment of the process. Us, not so much. We make the decision. To illustrate, lets say we live in a one-room apartment and we are sitting watching TV. On a commercial we look up and realize that we could not put one more dish in that sink with out the use of a hammer.

We decide to do the dishes. Without our realizing it we begin the "task." We look up. Surprise, were standing at the sink and the dishes are half done. For a moment we look at the dish we are washing and then suddenly we are finishing the last dish and making the decision as to what comes next. Perhaps we go back and continue watching the program. Actually we never stopped watching. Our mind continued to follow the television program.

While we were doing the dishes we entered a state of meditation. As we sorted the dishes we sorted our thinking. It was magnificent. Even though the part of the universe that did the dishes was our body, the washing up remains done by the automatic universe.

Boredom

The third of our trinity is boredom. It's gotten such bad press. Boredom is just the down stroke in our creative process. Rest is as important a part of the cycle as any other. It marks the change points.

We are thought to think we are experiencing boredom. We are not. This is just the setting of the stage for the decision that is about to arrive. Boredom is synonymous with accomplishment. They are inseparable. What have you accomplished that you are so bored? And what's the new inspiration?

Illustrative of this is the Wright brothers. They ran a bicycle shop. Let me guess they became bored with repairing bicycles. Then one said, "Lets build a bicycle that flies." Every tool in the shop got swung and today we can fly anywhere in the world. Boredom is not a "sin," it is a gathering of prana.

Where ever we are there is a joy in it.

The Ascension Trinity

[Also Known As The Teflon Trinity]

Warning: The following article may do away with all pain for the entire rest of your life. Proceed at your own peril.

We came here to evolve. True of false? Yes true, now how do we do it? We evolve by having experiences. Experience is the vehicle of evolution. Therefore there are no bad experiences as they assist us in our developmental process. Therefore there are no good experiences for the same reason. There are just experiences.

Once life is seen as, "just a series of experiences," then nothing sticks. And nothing has to stick because if there is one place that the word guaranteed could be used, it is that we are guaranteed to evolve. It will happen and there never has been an exception. Even the word devolve just means run me through that again, it was fun (fun in the bigger sense.) We're reminded of a child who after a harrowing experience exclaims, "Lets do it again!"

Our first conclusion… everything just is.

Instead of recognizing this simple truth our language misspells this concept: justice. Come on that's just ice. It freezes things, it numbs, and it holds things in place. Once everything just is instead of just ice, we become free.

When we don't get this, when we take it upon our selves to do the balancing, the "getting even," we don't recognize the purpose of our universe. This purpose, the manifesto of our universe is to bring everything into balance. And in our attempts to "make" his happen, we become stuck just like the dinosaurs in the tar pit.

Lets say that there is some one parked diagonally across a busy street during rush hour. An enormous traffic jam is ensuing. As soon as this just is, you are the one car that goes around because you are not attracted, there is no evolution for you to get, you don't have a job there.

The enormous pile of cars collecting are held there magnetically, by a single word, and that word is, wait for it... "Idiot."

To point it out, the word "idiot," whenever we use it, we are the "idiot." Call someone an idiot and we are not recognizing that person as doing as well as they can and therefore we are the idiot. Even if they are being intentionally idiotic, they are still doing as well as they can. Were we to say, "How dare you!" Then we are the least informed person in the situation.

Move into the world of just-is. Nothing sticks and we effortlessly evolve into the beings we came here to become. After we have calmed down, after we have moved into this world beyond right and wrong, it may happen that something gets our attention.

In the event something does "stick," it indicates that this is the focal point of today's evolution, this is something that is part of our incarnational contract and we have agreed to get it.

This entire tome is dedicated to techniques of adaptation, change, balance, self-improvement, advance, growth, maturity, this is to say, evolution. We can now know, with a higher perspective. We can now see, that the only reason for something to "stick," is that it is the next piece of our evolution. The lesson *de jure*. We are now, becoming more ascended.

The something that does "stick," refers us to defining the specific nuts and bolts of our incarnational contract. The "Why is this so sticky?" It's always the current step in our personal development. Otherwise it wouldn't have been sticky. Then just laugh, it's funny because we got it.

Everything that happens is God's will. It's that God turned His will over to us so that we can steer the development of the universe. It's like He wound us up and set us free just to see what we'd do.

This application of His will is called free will. Another name for it is "middle management."

An enormous number of us are so entangled in the blame game that we blame God for the machine gun. No, no that was some profiteer that used their free will to manufacture it. Then some fearful bozo used their free will to fire it. And then it was some volunteer that used their free will to chose to end their life by being hit with it. It's up to us to be in charge. All of this remains categorized as the "just is."

The Ascension Trinity, a proof of the nonexistence of guilt. There is no such thing as a victim.

The Trinity of the Fourth Dimension

Illusion, Unity and Awareness

In order to logically present the Trinity of the Fourth Dimension we are first presenting a truth of 2012.

First, there never was a Mayan that said or chiseled "The year two thousand and twelve." This is our interpretation of an event noted, in the fractaling of time, known as the Mayan Calendar.

The Mayan came to our planet to give us the time map. To do this they showed us the cycles of time that are related to the Earth spinning around the Sun as well as the Solar System orbiting around the Galactic center. A cycle, a spin around the Galaxy according to the Mayan takes fifty-two thousand years.

This divides neatly into four thirteen thousand year cycles. There is endless proof of this in the Earth herself. Every time she starts a new cycle her magnetic poles shift. A British gentleman did extensive work with core samples of lava. As the lava solidified it aligned with the North/South orientation of the time. His work revealed that every thirteen thousand years, the poles shifted. This shift has been going on for some time. We've personally measured a sixteen-degree shift in our very living room.

For the preceding four shifts, we have started civilization again from scratch. This time it's different. We will not be nukeing our selves back to the Stone Age. We will now be forming an advanced civilization.

Were we to have ended our current civilization, it would have happened at the moment of the first Gulf War. Witness this thinking. Saddam, declared war on the United States and owing to early senility forgot to buy an atomic bomb. No… He couldn't afford one? Hock a solid gold toilet? Oh, wait, it was the arms merchants, owing to their extremely high moral fiber would not sell him one? Not!

Saddam had a bomb. It was set off at about five minutes after midnight on that first day of the war. The fission was reversed by extraterrestrial engineers. Advanced civilization, not Stone Age, this is us. Thanks E.T. This is quite a crux because we are going to build an advanced civilization. The thing is that we are addicted to "failing." Yet, we are changing.

This Galactic orbit is elliptical. The year 2012 is the apogee, the point that is the furthest away from the center. After this point we are headed back home. The warming of our planet and the flux in the ozone layer is a natural part of this cycle. A few other things happen as well.

There are certain stars that are called photonic stars. They are connected to the central galactic sun by a light umbilicus. They spiral on the end of this light cord and "tell" other stars how to configure. Right now we are eight stars away from our photonic star. After 2012 we will be second behind a newly appointed photonic star, Sirius.

This new configuration is a promotion for our planet as well as the civilization on it. It is a promotion from third dimension to fourth. Once we begin to think in trinities it will be possible to lead more of a three dimensional life. It is within our experience to skip grades, to advance suddenly, even over night.

John Major Jenkins wrote a major book called *Mayan Cosmogenesis 2012*. He suggests that this mile marker is noted by some seemingly subtle changes in our local universe. At the present time, looking at the western horizon at sun set, one will see the planet Venus rise, then followed by the Pleiades. After 2012 this will reverse.

As far as the Gregorian calendar goes, there are those that have noticed that it was so poorly designed that it was corrected several time. This correction amounted to embezzlement. Since the Gregorian calendar was officiated by Pope Gregory we can assume it was the church that did the embezzling.

Can you hear the Pope saying, "You don't deserve a new year, repeat the year sis-six-six again." There are those who say this commonly used calendar is so inaccurate that the year 2012 occurred several years ago.

Lets take a look at the actual day, the event of 2012... We'll start by remembering the year 1000. Everyone thought that this would be the end of days, that the first day of the second millennium must be Judgment Day. And so all the last day of the year 999 merchants gave away their goods. The Pope made a fortune selling "Get out of purgatory free cards." And women, lets just say, "gave away their goods" as well. By noon of New Years day there wasn't even a storm. The pope suicided and soon enough business was once again, as usual.

Next let us consider the year 2000, did planes fall out of the sky and land on your foot? Do you have a garage full of food, batteries and an un-opened generator? The moment 2012 will more than likely lack that Hollywood drama we have all come to expect from the media driven early Twenty First Century society in which we are immersed. The principle we are suggesting is in looking back on it, like the Harmonic Convergence of 1987, it will have had a visible effect. Just not an immediate one.

One more logical proof: Doomsday Prophesy? How is this possible when there is no such thing as a victim?

The point is to let you decide for yourself. Do you feel that your consciousness has advanced to the point that it has begun the exploration of the advanced dimensional realities? Is time a different construct? Has bi-location become attainable? Is a clear mentality within personal power? Have you begun this transmutation into someone new?

The Fourth Dimensional Trinity

Drunvalo in his book *Ancient Secrets of the Flower of Life* points out that we the human race, are designing our selves to live simultaneously in unity and duality. This is a universal first.

The study of his book causes, caused me to recognize good, evil and unity as being three elements that are therefore a trinity. This trinity is an open door to the fourth dimension.

This is because when we observe this trinity (good, bad and unity), we establish the fourth point. The observing is the fourth point. In other words, the two dimensional trinity or triangle, becomes the three dimensional tetrahedron when the fourth point is established by our observation. Triangle to tetrahedron is literally a dimensional shift. This is the access point to the fourth dimension.

We can then exist in more than one system of belief simultaneously. One belief system is duality. The second is unity. The third is both together and the fourth, understands reality from this perspective. One paradigm engendered by the other. What joy, what Godlieness. Thank you Drunvalo.

The Quinary of Evolution

The start of a higher state of consciousness involves the shift into, the watching for, the thinking in and formatting in, sets of threes, the trinities. This is definitely so. Once this starts to become a standard in our thinking, there are even more exciting avenues of exploration.

Namely our advance into fourth dimension. Always there is more, always. Every atom in our universe is on its way to become its own universe. Have no trepidation; you've already created a personal universe, far distant in time and space. We just happen to be focused in third dimension, here, now and at this moment.

Five Fingers and Our Evolution

It may be noted that humanity is teaching nature to lie, as in genetically modified organisms (GMO), artificial flavors etc. Still it remains that the natural world doesn't lie. Any concept visible in nature is therefore true. We are aware that, if it looks like a pine tree it doesn't turn out to be a birch tree that cross dresses, or cross barks or however one expresses this concept. Nature is truth.

By this we can recognize our five-fingered hand as truth of the natural world and as a preexisting pneumonic as well. All of this puts the five elements of evolution right there at your fingertips.

All experience has an eventual byproduct, which has been referred to as natural selection. In studying this process let us call the smallest finger the first element, the experience. The pinkie is the event.

This fact is then quantified by language and stored in the memory. The ring finger can stand for the subsequent series of changes, the remembering. In this digestion of reality the next transmutation is called knowledge.

This unrefined knowledge seems fittingly assigned to the middle digit. We are prone to draw our attention to unprocessed knowledge by use of the middle finger, especially while driving.

The filtration of the knowledge results in wisdom. This we will ascribe to the ever so popular index finger. We are all aware of the wise use of the pointer finger.

Finally the thumb represents the actual evolution. In Palmistry the thumb, the way it is formed, is an indication of the use of will by the individual possessing said thumb. Use of will and level of spiritual advance are kindred.

Synchronous, yes? Easy to remember, yes?

Amnesia and Its Part in Evolution

Here is what you have in common with all other beings who refer to themselves as sentient. At the moment that God realized that as long as God was everything there wouldn't be much in the way of useful feedback. As stated we all have a right to our feedback.

At this moment of revelation God saw a whole lot of little hands went up and there was a rousing chorus of "Me Boss, Me Boss." An out take from *Fantasy Island* ? No it was the sound of you and I volunteering for this mission.

Since we all have to be God, no matter what, we're God... We did the next best thing. We agreed to forget that we are God. Welcome to the planet Amnesia and in some cases the United States of Amnesia.

This amnesia establishes, that is reestablishes the concept of innocence. We know nothing and yet we are capable of remembering everything. From the *tabula rasa* to a state referred to as wizen is the probable flight path through incarnation.

Normally innocence is beaten out of us and wisdom into us via guilt. This does not have to be so. Realize that this naivety is the effortlessness with which a child goes on to the next adventure in play. The past is not dragged along for the ride.

Understanding this and the instant forgiving, the actually loving oneself is easy. Our concept here is to get the wisdom and then renter this state of being carefree. This resets us and makes us fresh for the next experience.

Reincarnation, remembering everything from scratch again and again, results in a continuous up-grade. This is the same process by which we make a new model car every year, the redoing it, improves it. Congratulations on taking such a bold step as to have incarnated. This rights of passage that all of us go through is contracted so that we personally and the universe itself can move forward.

To review: Little finger, event. Ring finger, memory. Medius, knowledge. Index, wisdom. Thumb, level of advance. Associate our evolution with the five fingers and then all this will be handy (ha-ha.)

Don't stop here. It is a fascinating search. What other concepts fit neatly into our physical bodies. The Mayan calendar includes twenty tribes, one for each finger and toe. When something reveals itself as synchronous with our body it is a natural and therefore worthy of note.

Protocol Affirmation: It's easy for me to see inner dimensionally.

Protocol Four

<u>Guilt Puppetry</u>

*"An Idea that is not dangerous is unworthy
of being called an idea."*

Oscar Wilde

When it becomes necessary to initiate a self empowerment protocol it is because we have fallen asleep and are acting like a guilt puppet.

To think or feel guilty involves an inherent loss of freedom.

What makes the world go round? Love? This is a correct answer. Everything turns out to be love. There are other correct answers and one is guilt. More of this guilt is making the world go around than the majority of us would care to take a look at.

Subtly over a lifetime that love and adoration we have for the world is replaced by guilt and its cousin obligation. How did this happen? When did guilt take over?

Pre-Guilt/Native Human Ability

We human beings are born with some nifty stuff. In this section we are going to look at some of it. Soon enough, these powers are taken away from us. Firstly is the ability to "be." In fact, lets see someone not be. "To be or not to be," was a trick question. As the 21st century progresses we are becoming less human doings and more human beings.

Native to this state of being, is the ability to self-correct. We all have it. Have you ever found it necessary to tell some one not to stick their finger in the fire? Never, this is because we get that one early and it's instant. Fire, finger, fate complete.

Somehow, the waitperson has to explain that the flaming piece of flesh on the plate is hot and advises us to be careful not to burn ourselves. They do so in order not to be yelled at by the boss, lest the company is sued by a disgruntled and burnt customer and subsequently the waitron be terminated. Guilt is the motivation for the waitperson to act as if we are remarkably dysfunctional.

Here is a fun one. Ever burn your tongue on a hot cup of coffee/tea? Are you mad at the beverage, yourself or the person who gave it to you? You are mad at yourself because your self-correction mechanism had begun to corrupt. Fix it. It's our defense against the tsunami of guilt that we live in.

This negation of our ability to **self-correct** takes away another essential human power, the power of **self-reliance**. As these guilt behaviorisms spread, infect us, we look to someone else to tell us what to do, how to think.

Owing to this installation of guilt we can no longer rely upon our own authority. When you dress who decides how you look? If that person is anyone other than your self, say, "I now authorize myself to do anything that makes the heart sing." Now say it again. Now sing it!

"Walk Like an Ascension"

The second part is the ability to access the big picture. This is done in order to know how to act down here in the small picture. Each of us being able to get the larger image for ourselves, is our right. The byproduct is that it creates individuality. This is a real and really keen ability.

This access of the big picture is taken away from us by use of the term "daydreaming." It's brought home in the form of a report card. This accuses us of not paying attention in class, thus daydreaming. Enough of this and we tend to void this intrinsic instinct to know what is going on.

An adult word for daydreaming is **meditation**, although as an adult I love to daydream. So lets just call daydreaming the un-official meditation or playing attention. The restoration of our ability to meditate is the byproduct of clearing guilt out of our lives. One cannot meditate and be guilty. The Guilt makes way too much noise. This conclusion is simply observation and reason.

This lack of meditation, this inhibition of mental focus, may be spoken of as the vanishing of our capacity to know. Without knowing, our understanding falls into jeopardy. With no one knowing, shortly we morph into a society of slaves, each of us just doing what we are told to do in order to escape being punished as in: We the Sheeple..."

In the reintroduction of our ability to access the big picture, we automatically remember how to meditate. This engenders character. The more one meditates the greater the personality one has.

Another way to say this is, the more one meditates the more one enters a guilt-free paradigm. There is no "doubt," no "should," no "lack" in the big picture. We are all, realizing it or not, on this rout to greater comprehension. Witness, were the master to act guilty he/she would no longer be the master.

A path that we are all walking is called ascension. We will not ascend by: "needing, shoulding, trying, canting, recanting, regretting," or for that matter acting in any way guilty. I'm not guilty for being on my path.

A brief discussion of meditation involves trust. Just get comfortable, access your ability to feel love (picture something that is lovable). Now just say, "Show me the big picture." Trust that whatever comes to mind is the big picture.

Then say show me a bigger picture than this and keep on going until what ever happens is recognizable as love. If it isn't love it isn't the big picture. Now give your self-permission to believe it. We all have this facility, it is our birthright, reclaim it for yourself.

The **charisma personality** is always based of a loving attitude. In fact, if something looks like it isn't love, the name for whatever that is, is duality. Guilt, although not actual, is capable of souring us to the point that we destroy love we have created. We are so powerful that we are the only things capable of destroying love. How's that for the power of free will?

"Three, Two, One, Recognition"

Our third gift is the ability to **recognize**. Our human mind/heart/gut is designed to do this. It's what we are skilled at. In looking at any unknown, ninety percent of our initial examination is dedicated to identifying a face, any face. This is to say that we will first seek to see other people and then look at what they are up to. We easily recognize people, places, patterns and a lot more.

We are taught early on to give up our ability to recognize. It is from turning the authority, that is the ability to recognize, over to others. So, instead of reacting, we freeze because there is no internal voice saying, "That's danger lets get out of here."

Stalled by powerlessness, we wait for some alpha to get around to telling us what to do. This makes it, "safe" for us to act. Not very individualistic eh? Actually, if it weren't for all this instruction on what not to do, all those bad asses in high school would not have a clue. Well, they really didn't have any idea. They were just good at seeming like they knew what to do.

Still it gets to us when we don't become aware of something that is right in front of us. The eight hundred pound gorilla in the room is always guilt. This is the guilt over not discussing whatever the gorilla stands for. Start discussing and we have begun to become guilt free.

All manipulation is guilt manipulation.

Often we don't recognize guilt. Therefore we are easily manipulated by it. Were we to recognize guilt and then refuse to act guilty we could not be manipulated. It is this simple.

Another word for recognition is knowing. Knowing is always the first casualty of guilt. If we are in a state of guilt we don't know it because we don't recognize it. What else we don't know is that we are divine, that we are beautiful, that we are sovereign. There is a lot we don't know... yet.

Eatch for Falling Rocks

What knowing is guilt taking the place of?

Guilt replaces knowing. When you notice that you feel guilty ask your self what thinking is being replaced/deleted while this guilt marauds your mind. What is guilt taking from you?

As summation: One, not having our ability to self-correct destroys self-reliance. Two, not having our ability to see the big pictures destroys knowing. Three, not knowing destroys our ability to recognize. Many of us are occupying this level of consciousness, without knowing it. This doesn't have to be.

Symptoms of Guilt

Guilt is feeling badly. This may be feeling badly about something that has already happened or is happening or may happen. We are so powerful that we can create guilt about something we have not done yet. Even if it is from the future...

Guilt is always looking back.

This feeling of guilt is not a conscious feeling for very long. We vanish it, as it is untenable and it goes deep fast. It becomes rancid, affecting everything. We don't even recognize ourselves as the source of these unpleasantries. None of us care to hang out with people who feel guilty.

Doubt, is another indicator of guilt. Doubt as guilt, is the great destroyer of intuition, telepathy and a huge number of naturally occurring psychic abilities. We have the gift, we doubt the information, because of habit yes. A deeper reason is the idea of being guilty for being talented. Backward, Yes?

Using guilt as motivation? Clever? Not so much. Do something because it brings you joy. This is true incentive. Usually we are doing something in order to not be noticed, derided or admonished.

This type of impetus, acting to avoid being in a negative situation takes up way too much of our precious attention. There are no negative situations, unless we think negatively. We are all brighter than our behaviorisms. Hence the cliché, "Do as I say, not as I do."

Yet guilt still motivates the majority of us.

Which has lead to the...

The Guilt Epidemic

Once the brain recognizes something as normal it keeps it coming around. You know, repeat offenders, speeding in a car, chronic illness, smoking, over eating; guilt is the magnetic field that keeps these behaviorisms in place. Guilt has reached epidemic proportion and it's simply invisible.

We understand that our current language is binary. It's like a computer language. It's on or off, it's one or zero. The concept of criminality exists only as an opposition to moral behavior.

Guilt is like this, on or off. We exist constantly measuring, guilty or not guilty. The thing about guilt is that turns on and then doesn't turn off, at least not yet. Many of us feel guilty about things that happened years ago, even though we were doing our best, even though we paid for it. We are going to change this, which will end the guilt epidemic. This will be accomplished by installing a greater consciousness. A greater consciousness comes with greater concepts and a new attitude.

Five, Soon to Be Apparent, Guilt Manipulations

The wonderfulness of you and the skill to write new programming in yourself and your life is the truth. The ability to recognize guilt behaviorisms is an important tool. Reading this is developing this new sight.

Victim Guilt

This form is very common. It is the ever infamous, "poor-me." The whine tone puts the guilt-ee to sleep and one suddenly finds themselves attending the agenda of the guilt-er. Watch for this, whenever anyone starts listing everything they have ever done for you, they are angling to make you a minion. When they hit you with the new "favor," just say, "I will not comply. You are capable of taking care of this." Take the bate and you become the beta.

Martyr Guilt

This is a variation on the Victim Guilt Manipulation. Here the person pretends that they are hurt by someone or something, probably you. When all the while there are no victims and they have hurt themselves. They search for people who are conditioned to feel guilty when they "understand" that someone has been hurt. How exciting? No, it's way to common.

Then the martyr proceeds to tell anyone who will listen about this "injustice." This telling is commonly called "complaining." Anyone who responds to the complaint is milked like pregnant cow.

Please observe that the complaint is the command to keep the situation in place. And so the martyr/drama queen goes on merrily, until all those around them are used up or won't respond anymore, or have died. Put a stop to this. Call these people on this behavior. Do not give in. All of us have one hundred percent of the resources to create anything on our evolutionary life path.

Certainly we would be compassionate enough to listen, the first time. When it reveals itself as a pattern, the more loving thing is to direct their attention to it. Everyone is entitled to see themselves from other view points.

Happiness Guilt

This is the idea that if you are happy, or getting your share, someone else will have to do without. Nonsense! Not only is there plenty for everyone, all one has to do is decide. Again each of us has all that is necessary for the completion of our contract. Be happy it won't hurt anyone or you. Happiness guilt is an extension of lack mentality. We've all heard it, "Don't Worry, be happy."

Survivor Guilt

When we go through an experience that others do not survive either physically or emotionally there is some deep psychological, subconscious programming stating that we do not deserve our life. Again this is the idea that we took a "wrongful" share.

Survivor guilt is an extension of the comparison game. No one ever wins when they compare themselves to "what could have been." For this matter, "What will have been," as well. Remember that everyone chose their particular role in the event. This includes you. Think about it, you may have been the one that chose to come out whole, in order to tell the story. Self-love, we are all entitled to it!

Laziness Guilt

This one is cruel. It is the measurement of oneself according to some external standard. Again it's the comparison game. All the while the standard is internal. Little known is the fact that each of us is always running at one hundred percent efficiency. We cannot be "lazy." We are constantly where we are suppose to be, doing exactly what we are suppose to do.

Universal Edit

Didn't do something? It's because it isn't time yet. Missed an appointment? Call it "universal edit." It's always on our side. Some internal conflict is preventing the manifestation. Do not be guilty about it. Guilt will keep the information about this misdirecting conflict from being visible. I'm not guilty, now what's really happening?

Universal edit came to mind when I was due at an event, and had forgotten about it. I rushed and rushed to get there, only to find that the event had been canceled. It had slipped my mind owing to the universe editing my memory.

The very concept of laziness gives up its power to an outside force. There are no outside forces. We decide everything that happens in our life. Lets act like it. Lets remember that no matter what is going on it is the next step in our evolution. Therefore we cannot be guilty because of it.

I'm not guilty for being on my path.

What is the incentive for Guilt?

When we are that small child, and guilt is replacing our knowing, reason and feelings, we find out just how much juice (attention) there is in guilt. Since we have been cutoff from any true source of wisdom, namely ourselves, this juice is appealing.

Picture this small child sitting playing with their action figures, be it Barbie or Transformers. The child peers out of this world of their own creation, this world of their own attention and sees say mommy or daddy or any adult.

This person isn't doing much, just talking on the phone. Said offspring decides to get some of their attention, as it does not seem to be in use. In interrupting someone who is on the phone, this child gets a boatload of attention, all be it negative attention, yet a boatload.

It is your and only your attention that counts.

This is the name of the game. Until we educate ourselves and the next generation with the fact that attention is a sacred thing. Guilt will continue provide the incentive for all crime and immoral behavior. Validation counts only when it is internal.

The incentive for guilt is to get attention.

Re-think, re-train, re-programme.

There is no such thing as Guilt!

The universe will do what we tell it to do. Understanding this, certainly we can use our free will to make it appear that we are victims. Where there are victims there is guilt.

The most commonly used word in the news media is the word victim. We would suggest that it just be shortened to "V." Appearances are one level of understanding. They aren't the only level. Cut to the chase...

Because there is free will there is no guilt. The person, who is hurt, has made the decision to be hurt. The world is actually a perfectly choreographed dance of agreements. A victim is a fiction.

We are free to do anything and all we ever do, is choose what we are doing. Whatever someone chooses to do something we choose whether or not it affects us. Free will is a most amazing faculty.

Three types of people attend any war. They are: observers, participants and people that use the opportunity to call for their gate into other realms. There are definitely no victims and in spite of the concept of a "draft" everyone volunteered to go. Why did these people choose this? To have the experiences. Remember, the experiences will lead to wisdom and the wisdom will lead to evolution.

This concept of taking emotional responsibility, for what some one else has decided to create, is yet another definition of guilt. We have had the tendency to torture ourselves with this concept. This reality of being hurt by another is an inverse; it is always we who hurt ourselves.

Guilty up or dummy down

In the establishing the concept that we choose everything, we are well on the way to being guilt free. What anyone creates is their choice. We may choose that their creation impacts upon us. This collision is, and remains exclusively our decision.

We cannot be hurt unless we make the agreement, and then it is us who are hurting ourselves. Even if it looks like someone else, we are all one thing. The "other" is still part of us.

Victim or free will, choose one and be consistent.

Someone may choose to be hurt by whatever someone else has done. It is their choice. This "victim" has chosen this experience because of programming. We all fall asleep and then follow the herd role of victim until we grow the *cohunes* to no longer fall asleep.

Replacing Guilt With Love!

Lets look at motivation. We move away from something because it is unpleasant. You know: job, pay bills, not evicted. Or we move toward something because it is pleasant. Again, job, money fun. Our point is that the world can run better on love than fear. We may not trust this yet. All though, it's a comin'.

Stand on the world's tallest building and say I "can't" fly and the fear and the building own you and you're guilty about it. Stand there and say I won't fly at this time and you own your power. You own yourself.

Giant Chair

Eradicating Guilt

In realizing we are feeling guilty, we have taken the primary step. Remembering that there is no such thing as guilt, follows suit. Then it is time to reinitialize innocence. As for the reinitialized innocence, there are four letters "i" in initialize. Therefore it will have to do with I. Innocence means "in no sense." The etymology could have been "in no recognizable sense." As we grew older we began to recognize the sense.

Our concept is to find a moment in life where we were completely innocent. This moment is characterized by joy. Once we reinstate our ecstasy we just continue on without any thought of looking back.

Whatever is back there, whatever lesson is contained within any stimuli, any event, can be presented to us in the form of bunny rabbits and lollipops. Having it presented lovingly is courtesy of the use of free will.

The information is guaranteed to re-present itself. We no longer have to torture life's lessons into ourselves and therefore do not have to look back. It's the looking forward that deletes the torture. Guilt is always a looking over one shoulder, even if nothing has happened yet.

(2)

What about children? Those of us who are children choose our reality just as much as the rest of us. Every child chooses the experiences that specifically turn on, or turn off life's patterns. A molested child has chosen to turn down sexuality in order to turn up something else. For example, a career in law enforcement, black belt at age thirteen, etc. The experience was simply the most efficient way to do it.

This same child may have chosen this same experience in order to turn on sexuality. This was done because the pastlife history would have inhibited sexuality and the soul favored the exploration of it.

The "extreme" of the experience that we choose in life is precisely balanced with the resistance that we are designed to wage against it. Then there are no extreme experiences in one's life? Correct.

Each experience is precisely balanced with the amount of resistance, we will provide to the growth, offered in the experience. No extreme experience, then one mounted no extreme resistance. It is this simple. Nothing is actually turned up loud.

Eradicating guilt is about understanding our contract, all our contracts. When we allow every man, woman and child on Earth to take responsibility for themselves, and recognize everyone as being in the perfect place, it is just the beginning. As we understand other people's sovereignty, we are then in a position to see our own and vice versa. Everybody agreed to everything. Dance the fantastic choreography of free will co-operation on our beloved world.

Love as Guilt

Loving those of us who act guilty. We know that in a certain reality everything is identifiable as love. All things are love and this includes guilt.

When we do something out of obligation, love appears as guilt, even to ourselves. Resistance has divided this action, when it is motivated by guilt. We are beginning to see that we choose everything that we do. Guilt is an unnecessary factor.

In other words when we do something that we did not recognize as serving us, it looked like guilt and it really was love. When the motivation is worded as obligation there is a high level of resistance and therefore the guilt is functioning at peek efficiency. The guilt, not us. Guilt takes up a huge amount of brain space.

All motivation is love. All we do is love. It's a matter of knowing this. To stop the illusion of being driven by guilt, we can grow to understand, that...

We are the ones choosing everything that we do. Lets act like it!

The fact that we make the decision about what we are doing makes "guilt," irrelevant. Resistance drops out and we are free.

This is the example of how nonjudgmental love is and equally, how judgmental guilt appears to be. "Do this, or it means that you don't love me," this is just manipulation. If I love me, I may or may do this. The person, doing the doing, or not doing the doing, always selects the action.

Love of self is love of others

When you do something nice for someone else the world is a better place. When you do something nice for yourself the world is a better place. There really is no difference between the two.

As for our quest to release guilt as a way of life, we can spread this education/knowledge most efficiently by modeling for others. Send a copy of this book to someone you love.

Or someone you don't love.

Body of Guilt

"There are three kinds of lies. There are lies. There are damn lies and there are statistics."   *Mark Twain*

This section begins with this quote in order to introduce the idea of body of evidence thinking. If the only method of reason is body of evidence then we are in deed damned. Body of evidence thinking or statistical thinking is where we think about the odds of something happening, instead of will it happen or not. Whether or not something happens is decided by us, not "statistics."

We have said that guilt always takes the place of thinking. In this case it takes the place of thinking that's called third eye perception. This instinctive thinking is replaced by the statistics doing the "knowing" of probabilities.

The specific thinking that is neutralized by this body of evidence guilt is our knowledge that we are creating the reality of our life. This is rather than the idea that the outside is creating us.

(2)

The body of guilt is the guilt about the way we look or more specifically about the way we don't look. Lets start with the idea that we are at an AA meeting, only we are addicted to the way our body is supposed to look. Fun eh?

Stand up right now and say, "I'm (state your name) and I'm O.K. just the way I am. Be specific: I O.K. with my height, I'm O.K. with my hair color, I'm O.K. with blemishes, I'm O.K. with my skin, I'm O.K. with my sexual preferences, I'm O.K. with my age, I'm O.K. with my smoking. I'm O.K. eating an entire cow every ten to twelve months, I'm O.K. with my gender, and most of all, I'm O.K. with being O.K."

This accomplishes a reset. It is now not necessary to change and you will therefore stop unconsciously resisting change. This guilt thing has a real hold on us.

Twelve step meetings have done the world a world of good. The thing about twelve step programs is that they are missing the thirteenth step. What is the thirteenth step? It's the center. It's the you. The Thirteenth step is where you claim your power back again.

This is where the addiction no longer has the power over you. It's where you have the power. This is where you see yourself as the creator of your life. Power is defined as our ability to generate love.

The thirteenth step is the restoration of the human being prior to the addiction. It's the state of re-initialized innocence and wisdom co-existing. It's evolution. We are aware that former addicts are never the "same." This lack of restoration of the self is the reason why.

Everybody created the perfect body to accomplish the life's lessons designated for this particular incarnation.

What we don't like about our selves is the media motivated, deeply entrained idea, that there is something wrong with the body or its appearance. Stop creating your self by other people's standards. Find that moment of carefree joy that is you, your higher self, your true being and live there.

The amount of guilt behaviorisms associated with personal appearance (glamour) is astounding. This aspect in our society is a multi-billion dollar business and it is ludicrous. What if we all just stopped? What if everyone were just perfect as is? Would the world stop? What would happen? One thing is that our ability to recognize who people are will return.

In remembering our true self we may recall that moment in child hood where we said, Mom, I'm starving, my stomach is digesting itself. To which mom replied: You "can't" have anything you'll spoil your appetite. And the ever popular: mom I "can't" eat another bite, my stomach will explode. To which mom replied there are children starving in third world countries. Well that is a lot of guilt programming.

This is the point at we lost contact with a big part of our self-correcting mechanism. This part is called trusting your body to know itself. After this the clock runs us. Not just in the kitchen.

When it's dinnertime we become hungry not necessarily because we are hungry but just because the clock tells us it's a certain hour. We don't even know this. We are still children made guilty for being hungry.

(3)

On the web sight Telepathictv.com there is a list of classes one of which is called "Consciously Creating Your Life." After fourteen months of attending, one of the people walked right through all this food\guilt programming.

He said that one day he woke up and noticed he wasn't hungry. Even though everyone he knew seemed to "want" him to eat. Nonetheless, "I'm not hungry," was his only reply.

He continued on and found that even though the clock thought that it was lunchtime he still didn't feel hungry and so didn't eat. By dinnertime he still wasn't hungry and so he still didn't eat. In fact the entire day was spent without food but otherwise quite normally. Not fasting, not dieting, not abstaining, just not hungry.

The following morning he woke up and decided that indeed he was hungry. Of all the things he could eat he said that the only thing that appealed to him was a snickers bar. So that is what he ate. The entire rest of the day he was not hungry and therefore didn't eat.

The next day he awoke and in appraising the situation decided that he was hungry and of all the options available to him, a carrot was the only thing that appealed. You guessed it. He ate the carrot.

Change entered his life. He stated that, "Having an adult human body was like having a campfire. Every once in a while you want to throw a log on it, just enough to keep it going." Naturally he shed some weight. He wasn't fat to begin with. Everyone accused him as having a secret illness. He felt great, better than ever.

After some time and some weight loss he said that he had gotten over the guilt normally associated with food. No diet, no goal weight, no coach, no victim attitude and no guilt, without these influences his body just naturally went to its ideal weight. He did not loose weight he gained balance!

Simply decide that you are free of guilt about your appearance or the way you think or whatever and it will be so. We don't resist it, by being simpatico with it. When you don't notice, no one else does.

It's not who or what we are, it's the way we feel or think about who we are. Many years ago I found the most delightful linen tuxedo jacket, vintage fifties. I wore it to a rag. No one noticed because when I had it on, the way I thought, it was the sharpest jacket in the world. That was what people saw, the sharpest jacket in the world.

When the sleeves wore out at the cuffs, I noticed, and then so did everyone else. It was only because my belief about the jacket had changed that made it visible to others. It had actually been burnt for sometime.

You have the perfect body.

Accountable But Not Guilty

Dwelling in the reality that we are creating for ourselves is, quid pro quo, if this then that, cause and effect and so on. While all this is true it isn't the only truth. In this current epoch, before we truly remember our power, we tend to fall for things.

We love it or we "hate" it. It's just like our parents growing up. First we love them then we "hate" them then we love 'em again. We can be relied upon to be in one state or the other. It's less than fascinating.

We are here to create an intermediate step. No longer guilty or innocent, a third state. This new concept is of **Wisdom and Accountability.** This is a healed state that is to replace guilt.

As I'm sure that at some point the reader has thought "we can't have just everyone acting out whatever, it may result in...?" Correct, we are not yet prepared. Guilt still motivates us to do all that antisocial behavior. So we are each to become accountable for our actions.

Which is in line with the ancient concept called Karma. If we examine this karma concept, it insists that we will repeat every "mistake" we make again and again until we recognize the principle and self-correct.

(2)

Lets look at making a right on red, at four in the morning when there is no other car on the road and there is a "no turn on red" sign. Your authentic self says it's all right to turn, your guilty self says, "For god's sake don't."

Per usual we have to have an external authority validate any behavior. Guilt looks like fear and doubt. Your fearful self says there may be a cop, odd since there is <u>no other car on the road</u>. Your doubting self keeps you paralyzed until the light changes.

This is all because since childhood you've known how to cross the street and certainly know how to look both ways. But you don't act on your knowing because... face it, it's guilt. Yet there was no reason not to turn, none, nada, zip, zilch. We sat there for no reason. Come on.

The no turn on red applies during high traffic times but not at four AM. You are the only one who could make you guilty for going through it. If by some happenstance we were ticketed, we would be accountable for disobeying the letter of the law, yes.

Guilty? NO.

There is nothing the matter with making such a turn. Again the sign was designed to instill order in on a much more populated road. Again we are the only things on Earth that has the authority to make us guilty. The feeling bad, the feeling guilty over something, which wasn't harmful to do, is a habit, a habit that we can release. It can be replaced with the synchronicity of joy.

Guilt has long been stronger than logic. Common sense, or what ever we've got, it's the guilt that rules. What nonsense, are we ready to change yet? That traffic light is going to beat us to it. Change, we are certainly quicker than a red light.

(3)

The very big concept to get prior to the creation of the guilt free society is simple:

Guilt is the only incentive for crime and immorality.

When we tell a child that they are bad, and do this enough times the child feels: one, this is true, two there is no possibility of change and three, it is their duty, destiny to be bad and do bad things. Therefore their incentive is to be bad or "guilty."

It is understood by the child (subconsciously) that being bad will please the parent. Look, the child has been told they are bad. We as children are vested in winning our parents approval. Therefore the child must be bad, it's called incentive. None of this incentive to get attention changes, as we become adults, unless... There is reprogramming.

Spoken Guilt

"Argue for your limitations and sure enough they're yours."

Illusions, Richard Bach

At the present time there are what appear to be an enormous number of devices holding guilt in place. Actually there is only one, and that thing is you. This is to say, the way in which we think is not serving us. We think in words and these, now obsolete words, hold guilt in place. Guilt has us by the "words."

In declaring our freedom from guilt we grow an ear to detect the guilt manipulation. Yes it's a third ear, like a third eye and yes it is eerie. It will start the process of detecting the many words in common use that are nothing more than extensions, levers and devices that serve guilt.

"Self-Centered/ Selfish"

When we break out of the BOX LANGUAGE we hear people accuse us of being selfish when in reality they are actually angry that they no longer appear to control us and angrier still that they don't self-correct. Selfish or self-centered used to contain enough guilt anesthetic to put us to sleep and once asleep comply by acting guilty.

When someone uses selfish, just say, "What am I supposed to be you-ish? Funny I don't feel you-ish."

For self-centered just say, "If my center isn't supposed to be in me (self), where exactly is it supposed to be? Answer the question. Don't change the subject."

There are many common words and expressions that elicit a sleepy or guilt response. Never act guilty and you can never be manipulated.

When you take the bait, you become the beta.

"I've worked 'hard' all my life to get where I am today." This statement is guilt manipulation. It is true that it is a boast, a complaint, an observation, whining and a lot of other things but what counts is guilt manipulation. The subtext is that there is something wrong with you.

Well what's the response? Defending your self? That's acting guilty all right. If you say, "Ya me to." And voila you're set up as a minion. You never would have said that. Actually this is called fighting fire with fire which results in a bigger fire.

The original statement implies that you haven't worked all that "hard." In stating, "me to," the guiltification code was just muttered. It's not whether or not you've worked "hard," it is stating that you have. The statement makes the guilt.

A better response is no response. Then when they speak the manipulation just decline. You know, "How's that working out for you?" The word "hard," is in quotes because it is just one more belief/decision that is obsolete.

Another of these little guilt response mechanisms is "You've changed." This is the attempt to get you to do something you used to do. The inference is that there is something the matter with you now, so go back to the way you were when you could be easily controlled. "Everything changes." How's this for a guilt stopper of an answer?

"Not in the mood," means the something else that's the matter is actually guilt in the form of confusion. Asking what they feel so badly about is the inroad to the sacred yes.

Guilt clouds, feeling guilty always keeps us from finding our happiness. Until we find the answer with in ourselves, we have no useful information. We are each creating all of our reality. A popular idea, talked but rarely walked.

In all of literature perhaps the only illustration of not acting guilty is when Christ refused to say a word at his trial. All who would have defended him were told to remain silent as well.

This silence reversed the polarity and Pilot found himself defending Jesus. As soon as we say, "I didn't do it." We are acting guilty. Society defeated this one with the popular, "Silence means consent."

Have you ever noticed a person stutter or repeat the first word, especially when they begin a thought? This is a tell, it means the person is feeling guilty about what they are about to saying.

There is yet another form of guilt. Surprising? Sometimes unspoken guilt occurs in the form of body language. We recognize it when someone will not look up or makes too strong of an eye contact. Especially when they are speaking. Seeing guilt for fiction is one thing. Seeing the direct effect on the quality of life is a doorway.

Death by Guilt

"When you die in the wilderness, it's not from exposure, you die of shame."

Sir Anthony Hopkins spoken to Alec Baldwin, in the movie,
The Edge.

As we grow we get better. It remains as we grow older we become better. If you are ten years old you are appreciably better than any five year old on the planet. Likewise if you are twenty-five you are better than any eighteen year old. Forty and your better than thirty. Fifty and your better than forty and so on. Where is this magic line, where it's not so better?

It's age-guilt. We are so insidiously programmed with guilt that we don't grow old in the sense of development; instead we grow old in the form of shutting down. Actual physical shut down starts a few moments before the actual physical death.

A lot of us die rather than turn thirty, Jimmie Hendrix, Janice Joplin, Jim Morrison and these are just a few of the famous ones. This thinking about how un-cool it is to be over thirty is again age guilt. It seems to have copied into our current world paradigm. People in there twenties don't like (as a rule) people much older.

Just like any generation, if someone is older it looks like the parents telling, dictating what to do. It's the baby boom echo. How many of us work for people much younger? This is perfectly acceptable, unless we feel guilty about it. You know: "I wasn't recognized. That 'should' have been me." This whining just bleeds out our life force.

Lets take it a step further: Guilt and disease are synonymous.

All disease comes to remind us of some aspect of our development we have refused to get. Being remise in fostering our own growth is not actually possible. It is feasible that we are not yet aware of what our growth is about, yet our placement in the timeline remains spot on.

This guilt becomes disease when we continue to decline the movement forward, refuse to get the lesson. Someone desires time off from work but is too guilty to just call up and say they will not be in today. The guilt takes the form of the common cold and the day off appears. We could have just called in a "mental health day." Low self-esteem, self-hatred and feeling that others are better than us are all forms of guilt. As we become better at having love motivate us, instead of guilt, these things will fall away.

Have you noticed that we do not remember when the verdict comes back innocent? Well except O.J. but that's because no one believed it. Simple math, we are more interested in guilt than innocence. We are a society obsessed with guilt. How bright is this?

Guilt as the Puppet Master

"To tell the truth, in a time of Lies is in itself an act of revolution."

Oscar Wilde

Guilt is something worth keeping; check yes ☐ or no ☐ .

When a string is pulled the puppet moves. These strings, sometimes called aetheric cords, are invisible. They have been there since forever. Removing them is inevitable.

Guilt is a virtual oblige. It's not real but it looks real. We just "find ourselves," doing things. It's a bind. At this point if we act guilty and realize it, we feel badly. If we are unconscious and do something to avoid being guilty, we feel badly and, we don't know why. The Why? It's the only way we have been taught to think, that's why. Think a new thought.

Putting an end to this invisible master is our destiny.

Currently guilt is still the vogue. There is no system in place to hear, heal, remove, expunge, or assuage this diminishment of our abilities, called guilt. We are creating one at this moment. Remove the guilt by doing nothing that does not move the heart. Model this.

Forming the Guilt Free Identity

"A new idea is at first ridiculed, then violently opposed and finally accepted as self evident."

J. Robert Oppenheimer

The singular most effective way to undo guilt is the realization of just what a false premise guilt is. Since we've found that guilt takes the place of thinking then not being guilty would be described as **thinking**.

This is a "new" form of thinking. It is childlike. It is actually a much easier way to think. We keep referencing childhood because during those years we have not yet been taught to be guilty, well not as much anyway.

The recognition of the bewilderment of guilt is as a signal. Then becoming aware that the clouds are coming from this lack luster mind set. The flag goes up, do something about it. Some of us spend lifetimes in this muddle. Upon the comprehension of the veil of guilt surrounding us, one could just say, "Awake!"

A new identity is that of a person who knows that everyone is responsible for their own development.

(2)

Take a few moments to think. Imagine what it is like to be motivated by love with passion as the reason to get out of bed. This is as opposed to the current method, which could be described as, I'd better do it or I'll be guilty.

We can work together, assist each other, receive instruction and co-operate. We all self-correct. This process does not have to contain guilt. In GUILT WORLD all support systems are external.

This is how we are manipulated back into the box so easily. Crabs caught in a hole will actively pull the escaping crab back down into the "trap." Once we leave guilt world all support systems are internal, and others can still assist us.

Thought creates. This is a fact. The expression "It's only a thought," is useless. It's designed to keep us away from our true realizations. Before anything comes into existence it is first thought, well first dream and then it becomes a conscious thought but this is another book. Think free and be free. This is how it works.

Building The Guilt Free Society

Jelaluddin Rumi (Persian Poet from the 13th Century) suggested that there is a world beyond right and wrong.

We don't really have a model of a guilt free society. Sometimes primitive societies, who have not yet learned to lie, would serve as this model. They have already been dismissed owing to the use of the word "primitive." Even overlooking this there hasn't been a science channel program entitled "Guiltless Societies Around the World." These ancient philosophies are not championed in our caffeine driven malaise.

Getting rid of guilt will cause the world to fall apart... It's not true, another lie. Once we recognize guilt actually generates crime and immorality, we are totally happening. We have taken a major step forward.

(2)

We have a friend who made a t-shirt that said "Not Guilty." It was his observation that there were three distinct reactions. One their eyes went down, they would not even look at him. This is the person who is experiencing guilt as shame. They are completely dominated by it. Like all guilt and guilt reaction this is false.

The second reaction? Anger and not a little anger either. This is the "How dare you, 'pretend' to be free." Becoming angry is a common response to being invited to be guilty. This time it was an invitation to not be guilty. See this as a conditioned reflex, not conscious action.

The third was, congratulations, warmth, eye contact and a slap on the back. A big, "Atta boy." This is the self-evident part. "If Christ died for my sins, how come everyone still thinks I guilty?"

These three are society's reaction when we do not act guilty. As we leave the world of guilt manipulations, be prepared. Remember a first technique of maneuvering someone back into the box, is the cold shoulder. They look away, they ignore. Secondly comes insults like, "You're crazy." And thirdly your actions are accepted. As in, "Ya that makes sense."

Continue to search until we find ourselves as the cause of everything that happens in our life, in fact, the cause of everything in the whole world. If it looks like anything other than you is the source, then it isn't useful information.

(3)

The fact that the insurance companies are finally offering "No fault insurance," would indicate a first egress into the guilt free society. The reason these companies did this was purely economical. It cost too much to assign guilt. So guilt is useless and cost prohibitive? Yes.

Witness the enormous misdirection inherent in guilt. Society normally ignores the destruction associated with the chaos of guilt, except when it costs money. With the new sight downloading from this text, figure out how much guilt cost in the last year. Do the pie graph. What is the largest slice?

When first beginning to publish my thought was that in a few months, a year tops, the entire world would change. Now the realization is that this core level growth is to be staged over a number of generations.

What we suggest is to free yourself from as much guilt as possible and to raise our children as self authorized, as actuary adults. This is to say, beings motivated by love of self and love as others.

So far the only modeling of this is in science fiction. Star Trek puts forth the idea of a money free society in which all of us can be fully self-actualized. In this future, everyone naturally loves and supports everyone else. Universal love is the way it is, even though it's invisible, owing to the guilt encrusting it.

The guilt-free society will be a society in which no one is afraid of anything. Can you imagine the beauty in such a place?

Love is clearly a superior motivation. Think of each individual self-governing, all of us supporting ourselves as well as the whole of society. It's possible. It's an astronaut concept, as in seeing as the planet as having no borders. Also it's an evolutionary inevitability. Be that voice crying out in the wilderness.

It's Not About Guilt, It's About Authority!

Once we again possess personal authority, we will understand that we choose everything we do. The decision making we do, will be as a conscious faculty. Guilt will no longer be a part of our lives. All motivation will come directly from love.

Protocol Affirmation: I give myself permission to be authentic.

Protocol Five

<u>Placing Your Attention on Meditation</u>

In one reality our lives are an endless stream of very fine arts. One such art is, the art of placing our attention. As we have come to understand we create everything that is our life and we also create our attitude toward these events. In a sense, meditation acts like a buffer, standing between the event and the creation of the attitude about it.

There are many books addressing the subject of meditation. As a self-empowerment protocol it is excellent. The mind goes on in its constant response to stimulus, even when we are sleeping. We rarely ever recognize this. Instead we just react unconsciously to what ever happens to have set us off.

We have seen this. Just say, a few words from some popular song and that song will start singing its way through our mind. How would we stop it other than to let it wear out? We can have this much command of our thoughts. We can actually make the choice to cease it! Practice the "stop game."

An objective of meditation is to loose the chatter. This process may be started by simply distracting the mind by focusing on the breath.

Once this noise has stopped, one arrives at what has traditionally been called Nirvana. In the peace that is derived from such an achievement, there is a consciousness that is unparalled. When we quiet our mind, our soul speaks directly to us. Even without the full Nirvana one can still get information from places astoundingly on high.

An important factor in meditation is doing it regularly. Once it is done everyday one can build a map. This plan serves us well. One place on this map is an audience with the higher self that is observing our life. Everyday ask your higher self to tell you something about yourself. One day mine told me that, "One does not have to be <u>all</u> this thinking." Astounding, the amount of peace this augured.

Another subdivision in meditation is to talk to yourself about the events of the preceding twenty-four hours. Do you like your choices? Would you have made different choices? Talk to the spirit of your spouse or a friend in meditation and ask them what advice their soul has to offer you.

Another choice is to have a conversation with someone far more advanced than us. Ask them anything. Often such a being will pave the way for us to a much larger scope. I have found that sometimes there doesn't appear to be an answer. The brain just continues on with its day-to-day chatter. Actually, a wisdom may be recognized in the symbol language of the minutia. We are infinitely connected.

Divide meditation into conversations with as many different aspects of self as can be imagined. As a regular part of each day is spent in these higher realms the more effortless maintaining your cool becomes. Consciousness equals balance.

Bird Cloud

The Sustain

In the early nineties a picture called *The Shadow,* was released. Interestingly, for about half an hour after the movie, I could read minds and control traffic lights. The tutelage from the film had been this profound. Then it wore off.

What happens when we are elevated by the presence of the great teacher, our gain is good only so long as that energy field remains. It will fade, slipping us back into the amnesia. Understanding how the gain occurred will assist.

We have unlocked a magic door. Where this entrance is and how to get back there comes to us, as we get better in understanding our selves and the way our minds and reality works.

The subconscious is the part of us that may seem mysterious. Actually its job is to create reality and in the way we expect it to be. This movie rewrote enough code that reading minds came naturally. Telepathy was expected. This was such a departure from the normal subconscious patterning that it only lasted for a short while before the more permanent conditioning reasserted.

Well here it is. Making the exceptional normal. This is done the same way the normal became normal, repetition. Our subconscious mind is both, programmed by and creates, reoccurrence.

The more regularly we meditate, practice and stretch, the easier it becomes. The less resistance we provide, the freer we become. Doing something without resistance is called loving.

Protocol Affirmation: The consciousness with in me expands effortlessly.

Protocol Six

<u>It's Not About Anger...</u>

Anger has long possessed us. To free our selves from it, we must recognize it. Anger is not difficult to recognize. The healing begins when this anger is seen mentally as a <u>big red flag.</u> Yes, this does cast us into the role of big unconscious bull.

This flag is employed instead of the "coming to" later and the realizing of how destructive this behaviorism can be. When this flag is raised it sets off a diagnostic, a series of techniques that allows the participant to remain in create of their life.

First remember that anger is a blessing in that, it is the point past which one will not go. Becoming mad means you are unwilling to put up with something. This annoyance serves as delineation. In our current word it signifies a loss of control, when in reality, it is the acquisition of control. A small child will scream and by doing so creates an area around them that is temporarily cleared. This is the declaration of a border.

It's just that as an adult, it serves us well if this is kept internal. We all know this sort of hostility equals apology, restraining order, fistfight, lawsuit, frightened people, giving flowers, expensive gift etc. When the process is internal (flag/diagnostic) then true create and blessing come from our ally anger and its job is done by our diplomat.

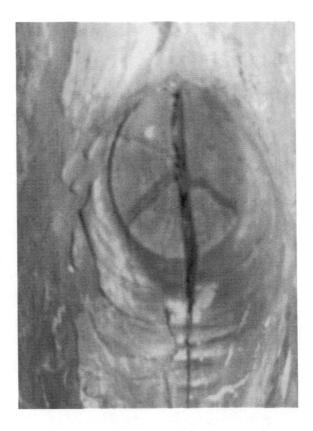

Anger as missing information.

"I'm so upset that what's their name is late." Missing information? Someone says, "flat tire," and the anger is all gone. Anger, all gone, say, by-by.

This missing information is always about the situation being different than it is being perceived. Process VS. Potential is another version of this universal concept.

Telepathy is capable of supplying the missing information. Just quiet your mind and say, "Show me." This truly psychic faculty is funded by our participation. All human beings are psychic/telepathic, there are no exceptions. We've just divided this ability by the amount of denial we have in our systems. More denial equals less psychic ability and inversely.

When we ask for the information to be delivered telepathically it will be. What ever is perceived will result in one of two things, doubting or knowing.

When we don't believe we continue to be upset or setup. Later on when the logical mind sees the truth of what we got, we spit out the cliché, "I knew it."

When the data is delivered through our knowing, we calm down. We chill when we believe, we fry when we think it's a lie. Make a choice here.

Anger as attachment to outcome

We are often putout because of the belief that we live in a world that isn't an optimum. Actually it is. We seem to have this idea of a smooth flight as the only ideal sequence of events. We are attached to this concept.

When this doesn't happen we assign blame, which shortly leads to anger. This sudden hostility is characteristically directed at anyone else but ourselves. The solving of this BLAME GAME is the recognition of our selves as the only source of this "conflict."

Source Consciousness

When there is no doubt left, when we can identify ourselves as the cause of everything that happens, we have achieved what would be called source consciousness. Any event, anything that happens has been engineered by us. This is done so in order to set the stage for the following rung on the spiral that's awaiting us. Until awakening, our powerless mentality, will eclipse this knowledge. Yet, the fact that we create our life will remain true.

Here's an example of how the blame game unfolds. Were in a store and be see the perfect thing. We have the money and it is the exact item. We don't buy it because doubt has seized us. A week later, after having resolved our doubt, we find that there out of stock.

In reacting by calling the manager, one is poised on the brink of the blame game. It was the doubt, not the manager. The doubt is easily understood as having been sourced in us. Not seeing this is the lit fuse.

It is only when we understand that we are creating our lives that we are in charge of them.

This knowledge is a way of life. The question never was, "Why did this happen to me?" The question is always, "To what does this provide effortless access? What lesson does this disguise?"

Angry Words and Self Reproach

When someone, using the words that escort us to the powerlessness of guilt, misleads us and then they proceed to manipulate us, it urinates us off pretty well. Either we deride ourselves for this or ask, "What am I still pretending to be guilty about?"

Once having identified the attempted guilt manipulation as the root cause of the anger, one is again in full creation of life. This is instead of being controlled by one's own unconsciousness and or unhealed emotions and recrimination.

Very often just saying "no," will take care of the entire thing. When the diagnostic has gone off enough times it just shortens to, "I am so happy when I remember that I am not guilty."

Not Choosing Anger

Something that we are "unhealed" about has pushed our button(s.) Another word for unhealed is "lesson." Look at the anger behavior as a selection, a conscious selection.

One choice is the common one, anger. A second possible decision is declaring borders. The third is the neutral stance, in which meditation/ analysis is the decision. As we grow we become better and better at seeing things for what they really are. Now choose one of the three.

In order to declare borders or meditate one cannot be guilty about it. Certainly, in choosing rage, one is already acting guilty or more specifically, reacting unconsciously. More conscious equals less anger.

Eventually it becomes, "peace equals boundaries." So anger is the choice between declaring boundaries or declaring war. Easy choice, yes? War every time, no? Oops sarcasm, but you knew so it's just humor.

How do we get to a higher level of consciousness? Ask for it. Keep asking for it. Ah, a little meditation wouldn't hurt either.

Diplomat V.S. Rebel

"Raise Your Hand If You Have Oppositional Personality Disorder. Oh, no I mean raise your hand if you don't have OPD." This is how I started a seminar/book signing in Columbus Ohio. Not a single hand went up. People did focus their attention and we had fun.

What we know about a person who is a rebel or diplomat is that they were raised by loving parents who were control-freaks. Oops, I meant to say micro-managerialy challenged parents. I mean parents that have leadership conundrums. These are parents who in the name of love and protecting their offspring, inhibit this child from finding borders, on their own.

Growth/maturity/evolution may be defined as the recognition and enforcement of borders. In this dysfunctional home, if there is even the most abstract possibility of danger to the offspring, the child may be physically/hysterically prevented from some activity. Often referred to as over reaction.

This may include although is not limited to, keeping the child from putting dirt in their mouth and thus developing an immune system capable of dealing with a perfectly normal environment. We are definitely in favor of nurturing the children of our world. Engendering an adult is the object of raising a child.

Being raised by control freak parents will result in the next generation of control freaks. Two things happen to these kids. One, they become experts at negotiation. This stems from a feeling of powerlessness fostered when the child has neither attitude nor vocabulary to advocate their role in some activity. Later they get good at it. As in, "I'll do it myself." And thus our second attribute is born, the rebel.

Within each of us there are these two personas. There is a master of tact and one steeped in opposition. As stated, the axiom of trinity is: When two things appear as opposites there is a third point of view, a third thought, that will allow us to recognize the two poles as the same thing. And so it is with the diplomat and the rebel.

The healing of this effect (trinification) begins with the examination of the tool belt of the diplomat. We identify thousands of tools all having to do with the art of communication. When we look at the rebel's tool belt there is only one tool, a nuclear bomb.

In the life lived as the diplomat/rebel one exhibits the ability to talk anyone into anything. At the same time we are a builder of lists of grievances. These complaints we discuss with no one. That is until one day, in a state to total disgruntle, we burn the place down like a boat on its way to Valhalla.

Now to cure this is to return to our examination of the diplomat's tool belt and the discovery of the very last tool, which is the identical nuclear bomb. Only after all negotiations have failed does the diplomat go to war. Anyone in business knows that in order to effectively negotiate, one is to be willing to say no, and walk away from the table.

In our life lived as part time diplomat and part time rebel there has never been a negotiation of the grievances. Every time the thoughts of opening the dialogue begin, the rebel shuts it down.

It's as though this skill in negotiation/diplomacy is halted. It reminds one of the child who has not yet developed this tact. The unhealed adult will hang on to these same slights as though they are somehow valuable and until they reach critical mass.

To start the healing, is to reintegrate the rebel and diplomat as one person. Start by calling these people who don't know that they are on the list. Sit them down and go over these points of distress. Make eye contact, communicate your side of it.

This may sound like: "Six months ago you took a pencil off my desk. I want you to know two things: One I don't care and two, It will never happen again."

Go over the entire list. "Hello, we went to fifth grade together and you did something horrible to me. I want you to know two things...

In hearing that you don't care, the subject knows that you are cool. In hearing that it will never happen again... Well, who wants to find out exactly what this means. They understand the last tool in the belt.

Do it. Clean up that list. Then once it is gone it is a new world. When another item would be presented that would join the list... It would not be tolerated for a moment. You'd begin negotiations instantly, then and there. Both are valuable parts of us, now we can recognize them as one, much more valuable, part. Enjoy your new life and your new power.

Protocol Affirmation: When I'm around the good times are to be found.

Protocol Seven

<u>I Am Bigger Than This</u>

Another word for paranoia is powerlessness. Whenever we take anything personally we feel powerless. Taking it personally is the cue for the reset. There is no place in the universe that we are powerless.

We live in a world where we are trained for low self-esteem and external validation. A ten year olds opinion of us may be more important to us than our opinion of us, how silly is this? By now we can easily remember that other people's opinions of us are actually their opinions of themselves. Knowing this is greatly freeing.

Which is bigger, your auric field or a tornado? Your auric field. Have you ever looked at the path of a tornado? Sometimes it crosses the street in order to not destroy one house. Then crosses again to continue right after the skipped house. It was the auric field of someone in that house.

Which is bigger, you or the Earth? You, because you can comprehend the Earth. The Earth is within your thinking and you are bigger than your thinking. You create your thinking. This is real.

Merkaba

Building The Dismissificator

Sometimes we humans get "caught," in an experience or idea that just keeps repeating in our mind. Stopping fictional thought is like any growth process. First, is to identify something as fictional. It is not true, and secondly, it is not some hidden piece of our incarnational advance, cleverly disguised.

Where this mindamonium to turn out to be something of value, then we deal with it. Then this tape loop is suddenly on our side. Seen, as a short cut to what is really going on, the authentic lesson, we are in the power position.

When these things come up in repeating mode and turn out to be worthy of note it is a cue/clue. The specific piece of forgotten consciousness, delineated by the tape, shows us the nature of our growth. The question becomes how many time does this thing have to repeat before we make the sacred decision to change?

We can spend hours down, beating ourselves up, because we stood up for our rights by speaking to a stranger in public, who was being out of line or was that cutting in line. There was a line, (a border) involved at any rate. The idea is to, forget about it, the person was asking for some external correction. Be proud of being the one who volunteered to do the job.

Another example is waking up with a feeling from a bad dream. This feeling goes away as soon as we realize that no matter what it looked like, it is a form of self-correction.

Equally instinctive is our desire to defend. Don't feel badly for having protected someone who could not do it for themselves. It is who we are. When someone is capable of defending themselves it is our sovereignty to allow them to do so. No matter what, it isn't possible to be in the wrong place at the wrong time. Every event, every moment in our life serves us well. It is a matter of recognizing this and loving ourselves because of it.

All muscle is built by the use of the muscle. How do you get to Carnegie Hall? This new power to discard, that which does not serve us, is simply changing in subject in the thought stream. Have a stand by, pleasant thought, ready to continue the flow, once you have dismissed.

Whether this repeater thought is doing so because of habituated guilt or because it is a hidden advance, is the key. Consider that it may be that the habituated guilt is the lesson. We are becoming greater at conscious change.

Our thought is a powerful and sacred thing and we are its creator/master. Where this loop to return, give it a second brutally honest look. Still nothing worthy of attention? Good, in the event that it comes up again, perhaps a day or so later, analyze it again.

Write some advanced thought patterning. Release the old patterning, it's gone. Pump this puppy until this new strength becomes automatic. Hit the Dismissificator until it is a personal faculty.

Strength

It's not about strength, it's about focus. It's the principle of any marshal art. This is a worthy proponent of human power. Begin with the question; is generosity an attribute of strength or weakness? The answer is strength, great strength.

This is because in order to be generous one first takes care of oneself and then one is in a position to take care of others and to be generous about it. True strength is inherently from grace.

Another very interesting concept is to observe the number of time line dimensions that are crossing in our world at this moment. To examine this lets look at the archetype pirate. This is, live by the sword, die by the sword. Not too many pirates these days. A lot of inner city gangs, it's the same thing. There reality is not in our reality.

We live in a different dimension than these urban pirates. This other reality crosses ours although it is not part of it. Therefore we could walk right down the middle of a turf war, surrounded on both sides by rival gangs and never be hit by a slug. In fact the bullets would go out of their way to miss us.

This is because we are not in their dimension. We wouldn't even be visible to them. Note that fear could modulate us down and then we would pop into their frequency… unnecessary.

As we suggest on our show and in all of our classes: it is time to regain our sovereignty. Decide to live in this way. And not, ah sometime, next week maybe, I think perhaps, as soon as I have discussed it with other people, oh eventually. There are the dishes to do first then… Decide to reinitialize your sovereignty at this very moment.

Deciding this is the beginning of a lifetime process. Not making this decision has a name, is called normal. This decision is the potential of the super-natural.

The protocol… Take a composition book, like the ones for kids and fill it from cover to cover with, "I am sovereign of my reality." Do this.

Getting It

We so easily forget. There is nothing that isn't simple, once we understand it. The distance between us and getting it, is the IDEA, that there is this distance. There is no distance, there is only us, only our beliefs.

Decide that you can understand whatever this is. Pause, and then re-read and then, as though by magic, understanding. This technique does away with the low self esteem paradigm that we have come to refer to with the word stupidity. Relief is belief.

Protocol Affirmation: There is always more edge to cut.

Protocol Eight

<u>Reprogramming Fear</u>

In our growing understanding of the universe, in it becomes apparent that the concepts of good and evil are things of the past. Leaving with them is a large number of vocabulary words.

Dear reader, please excuse the number of words that do not serve us in this section. These outdated words are used to mark obsolete concepts. They are often in quotes and their use is just to direct one's attention toward the growing discard pile of the old belief systems.

Another important reminder is, as we have stated, we do create 100% of our reality. The illusion is thick at this point. So one will realize that there is no such thing as a "fear contagion," even though it sure looks like it. Our objective is to facilitate the growth past our programming. There is nothing outside of ourselves.

Lets start by remembering that fear is virtually invisible. Partly this is due to the fact that it comes in so many disguises. Worry, doubt, guilt and regret are synonymous with fear.

Fear and powerful thinking are by their natures mutually exclusive. While fear may appear to induce wisdom it is really just habituating anxiety and diminishing the fresh approach.

It's Not About Fear, It's About Consciousness.

Picture yourself living a bucolic life in an architecturally astounding monastery, by a beautiful lake in the middle of an old growth forest. Frolicking freely yet always surrounded and supported by our fellow seekers of wisdom. With such a creation one would be given to feel empowerment, life! Prana collects in such a place.

Now picture a scene of urban decay, police sirens, automatic weapon's fire, angry people, a world where concrete is the only thing ever underfoot. This is an equally valid incarnational decision. Prana collects here also.

The difference between these two places is the presence of the true form of pollution, the fear. Because of the lack of valid education, it appears to spread. Once afraid others tend to copy our trepidation, a modeling that does not serve.

This is the habituated, "looking to others to dictate our actions." We will come to seek our own council first as we enter adult hood. Actually fear is fun and easy to do away with. Ever notice how someone will be frightened and then laugh?

We are all far more telepathic than is known. When a lot of people think the same thought in the same place it remains there. The next person to go there is likely to have that thought. Ergo, "thought form." We are more powerful than a thought form; it's just a matter of recognizing its presence. Any one of us can vanish a thought form as simply as deciding it is gone and then clapping our hands. We don't really have to clap our hands, it just makes it more fun.

Lets start at a beginning. Good place eh? Long enough ago man walked the earth in a true beauty. We created, walked and talked directly with God. We were in fact gods and goddesses. It is time to remember this again, immediately, at this very micron in time.

All fear has a single root cause. All fear is sourced with the belief in our own inadequacy. We are infected with this single idea: We are somehow incapable of dealing with… something. Nonsense, have you dealt with everything so far? Do you believe you will suddenly create something that you are incapable of taking care of? Again nonsense!

Fear is a lie, in fact the Big Lie, the lie on which all the little lies are based. The Big Truth is that you can handle it. We are evolving to the place that when we are confronted with a fear our brain will automatically say, "I can do this."

Pine Cones

The Seven Stages of Fear

The seven sections are each described by an individual word. This is designed to better enable us use our new ways of thought. In the follow through there is a more readily regained balance. When we recognize our self or another use one of these words, we can perform a reset in our thinking. Thereby we can gain self-mastery, which is always mastery of the situation.

1.) "Fried"

The fear enters upon our stage when we open our thinking to it. This may be caused by a large number of things, tiredness, low blood sugar, a phone call, a certain cinema, caught "off guard," your birth. In short, we may call this daily life. More specifically, fried means that a disproportional amount of life force has been used in resisting.

This is primarily because, fear, once it inculcates, makes us less able to think. Being afraid, takes up an enormous amount of brain space. Then we settle for an existence that is a roller coaster made up of misunderstood emotions with the blame game thrown in for good measure.

When you hear the epithet, "I'm fried," you automatically know that some one is overly tired, overly sensitive and could be told that it is all right to take a break. It's also acceptable to take a beak yourself. In fact, I'm tired/fried means, "Take a break." Compassion is the keynote response because we've all been there and know it from both sides. "It's all going to be just fine," will keep the downward spiral from continuing to spread.

To paraphrase Shakespeare, All the world is a stage and each of us plays many roles. Lets add three things to this concept. One props and costumes have great effect. People read the way we look.

"Always dress better than they do," is a quote from Steve Martin in the movie *Leap of Faith*, written by Janus Cercone, produced by Paramount.

Our second axiom is that, each individual writes their own script. So we would suggest writing a leading role. No matter how we write it we are playing the leading role in our life.

Bit parts don't add up to much at the end of the day. When we buy something form a salesperson, we may end up a bit player in their day. We are suggesting not to make that the only role we play.

Our third concept is timing. It's an important factor. When one is not yet ready to manifest something and one doesn't know this and then pits their will against their own subconscious, this process is called Willful Behavior. Willful Behavior is always characterized by frustration.

What we are saying is that life is lived in attention spans so, when one becomes fatigued, take a break (Timing). Remember self-discipline is a form of self-love.

2.) "Anger, Contempt and Sarcasm"

There is no anger there is only fear disguised as anger. Anger is a powerful master. The thing anger causes us to forget is that we are far more powerful a master. Observe, we create this state of anger in order to take over the doing of something that we've decided. This is usually an unconscious decision.

The rant may begin, "How many times have I told you…?" In this scenario, it is a feeling of powerlessness that is funding the hostility.

Whatever we are mad about, we have let it slide until we can no longer tolerate the situation. The emotion of anger signals the time for change. Seen this way, this annoyance can be a blessing and is therefore on our side. Then it's the now famous, "Make a different choice."

People who live lives of anger have stalled. They have given themselves the cue and at the same time haven't taken it. Anger without any education transmutes into addictive behavior.

Contempt

When one is in a state of contempt one is angry. This is directed at someone/something for not understanding or being in accord with our own life view. The healing here is the remembrance of when we were, ourselves this ignorant. In the external healing of the other, one might open by telling the story of the moment when we recognized these traits in ourselves and then made a resolve to advance. Then encourage them to take the initiative for them selves.

Contempt is always contempt for oneself. When we recognize this distaste about someone else, it is systematically about our self. This other self is from a different part of our timeline. Advising this other person, other self, and moving into the improved world is an effect better left to our diplomat. This rendering is always enhanced by our heart's compassion. Build a mental construct that automatically reviews when we were "that" way.

Sarcasm

Sarcasm, parody, satire and mockery are all humor attempting to buffer contempt. We will use the word sarcasm to represent all these aspects of anger.

When one teaches and at the same time uses sarcasm, their students may or may not get the lesson. Like so many human facilities, encrusting it in code, ultimately creates a greater reasoning ability. The immediate byproduct is always confusion. The student will not know if the teacher is serious or not.

It is the use of humor that is admirable. Knowing that everything serves us makes the transition from anger to effectiveness an effortless one.

Criticism/insult is always translated through the level of consciousness held by the one on the receiving end. An insult or criticism always reveals a very deep bit of information about the one hurling the epithet. At the same time it calls one's attention to another point of view. Valid or invalid, viewpoint is an important observation.

3.) "Bitterness"

Bitter equals the obsolete concept "disappointment." We get caught in judging of some event and then go over it again and again. We are unable to free ourselves because we have never been taught (reminded) how to do this. The actual definition of "disappointment" is: Things worked out perfectly even though it wasn't the way I thought they would.

Once we can recognize life as an endless stream of access points to fulfillment the bitterness washes away. Bitterness, like all symptoms of fear poisoning, keeps us out of the now. When bitterness is left without education, turns into the next stage which is...

4.) "Apathy / Depression"

But I don't care. (Ha-ha) Apathy is a defense mechanism. It's used to prevent commitment. It keeps us out of the game. When we aren't in the game we can't make a "mistake." Again the new definition of mistake: There is no such thing as a mistake it just another way of saying I took the scenic route. Looking at it in this way creates an educated perspective.

At the point called apathy, all the other human beings become excluded. Fear has successfully isolated us. The entire behaviorism "apathy" indicated a desire for some alone time. There's nothing the matter with this we all have a right to privacy. Unchecked and the real "dirty work" can begin. There is the possibility that only our pets can bridge the gap our fear has created between us and our own specie/life.

In hearing someone say, "I don't give a fuck," you have identified someone in the apathy stage. We may be able to pull them back in by simply saying "Yes you do."

Apathy sets up an internal conflict. It is our nature to care. When we are apathetic we are contrary to who we really are and the next stage sets in.

Depression

When someone who is apathetic finally commits to it, the result is depression. Depression is strangely enough indicative of growth. We have out grown the confines of the life, which we are living. The depression part comes when we do not recognize having ordered the old life to stop. Furthermore we have not given the command to start the new one. Depression is halting. This downward spiral is apathy applied.

The escape from depression involves taking the first step toward the new you. This is the you that is no longer restricted by the beliefs of the old you. The paralysis may end by sheer determination of will.

What might that first step be? There is quite a variety. What we can tell you is that you have already thought of it many times. It may be as simple as having your new identity printed on a business card. It is about you committing to yourself! Decide to begin your new life. Now do it.

Once this new step is taken the entire block of depression will vanish. The new life is now in the process of leaving the mental realms and entering third dimension. Once it starts it will conduct itself like a snowball rolling down hill. Congratulations.

5.) "Confusion"

The phraseology of the fifth stage is, I don't know, I just don't know. Confusion, muddle-headedness, doubts are all the byproduct of guilt/fear. We have acted/been acting against our own nature and therefore feel guilty. Here is how it works. Our nature is to be. And the byproduct of being is creation. Creation is characterized by decision/choice.

Confusion marks the "breaking" of the spirit. We no longer have the will to decide. This paves the way for the shut down.

At this point a spirit guide/ angel is recommended. This guide, this being's job, is just to remind you of what you already know to begin with. Call Clarity. Knowing is an interesting game. Knowing is our birthright.

Human thought is the immensely strong. We just don't know it. Watch closely... We know and then we doubt. It's important to notice the "then" part in that last sentence. This goes on all the time in our thinking, just notice. Knowing and doubting are about a microsecond apart. Knowing always comes first otherwise the doubt would have nothing to pit against. Confusion always reflects feeling fear/ guilt. Our power can be restored in any number of ways. The entire of this volume is dedicated to this idea.

Ask anyone, including your self, who is experiencing confusion to, stop, just for a moment. Now focus on something that you can see, that is the thing that is furthest away from you. This is a physical as well as a brain reset and it will work. The momentary pause breaks the hold and our resilient self, pops back up.

6.) "Terror"

We are torn up by terror. Prior to this the fear has been eroding us and we have fought against it. Once confusion set in we didn't have much left. Irrational fear grips the entire being and the stomach begins to dissolve itself. Our life force drains rapidly as we find ourselves in a dark future or tormented by fear in some other time slot. Either way we are clean out of the now.

Lets say we are sitting on our bran new white couch just delivered. Suddenly we have slipped into the idea that we may not be able to pay the credit card (fear). Unchecked, we imagine it being repossessed. Sweaty workmen smear grime all over it as they toss it into a filthy truck. You weeping uncontrollably, as the truck disappears toward the horizon. *Mon Dieu*, what nonsense. The couch is bran new and you are sitting on it. Come back now, to the now. Remember that you can handle it.

This is the opportunity to address the idea that we live in a thought stream and that we are sovereign of it. Recognize that one doesn't have to continue the dark fiction. Snap your fingers and halt the negative thinking in mid syllabray. The physical movement of the hand snapping the fingers instates a brain reset and gets the body in on it.

Now think of a pleasant thought. Fear is never in the present. There is only trick to fear is recognizing it as fear. Simply fear is a thought that makes you feel badly. Stop it. It isn't real.

Any thought that makes you feel badly is a fear and you don't have to think it. For the rest of life there doesn't have to be a thought that makes you feel badly. Something make you feel bad? Just stop it and now choose a happy thought, a thought that is worthy of your attention. You are sovereign of your stream of consciousness.

F.E.A.R. False evidence appearing real. The hippies got it right. Who knew?

7.) "Despair"

This is the famous, I Quit. We have names for it, resignation, suicidal tendency, withdrawl, chronic fatigue, laziness, catatonia, etc. It's the giving up. Actually what is going on is the final draining of life force by the fear.

We may have first experienced this as that small child who lost some game and then didn't want to play any more. It's exactly the same human reaction, old style human that is.

Elizabeth Kubler–Ross, has suggested that the five stages of death are: denial, anger, bargaining, depression and acceptance. Another system that fits on our fingertips. This is an interesting map as it continues running throughout our life, until we do something about it.

By way of humor they have finally translated the scream that new borns are so prone to. It means, "Oh, No, not again." Denial, yes? As young adults we become angry. The word surly is often used. As middle adults we bargain. The next stage may be characterized by depression and finally the acceptance that is old age.

Psychotic Break

The urban myth, "we only use ten percent of our brain," caught on so easily. Was it low self-esteem? Yes. Was it self-hatred? Yes. What was it really? It's that there is only about ten percent of our thought capacity that is available. The other ninety percent is keeping fear, doubt, worry and guilt active in our minds, we just don't know it.

Psychotic break means that, our normally diminished bit drive, gets over whelmed when someone says/does the smallest thing, like make a left turn. The brain, almost out of space, interprets this as more guilt or whatever, reaches capacity and crashes. You know, "You're getting on my last nerve."

The screaming associated with the break is the last power surge going through the equipment before the shut down. Then the rebooting begins. We can tell the brain has gone back up on line when we hear, "I'm sorry."

Psychotic break is our way of giving our overloaded mind a break. It indicates that the person would serve themselves well by beginning a self analysis about what is really going on.

We have all spent lives of "stress." Which is really only fear of disapproval. It is expectation. It is the desire to be in the future. Individually, we are the only ones, with enough authority to get us to think of ourselves as guilty, fearful, doubting or worrisome. Lets get a hold on this and reactivate our power to self-correct. Seeking assistance from others can put us in a position to start the process. Ultimately it is only our remembrance, our self-correction that will get it done. Tutelage from the other is really coming from inside the house.

Our Immune Response

Create your objective witness. This is the part of us that just observes. This allows us to see into which stage the fear virus has progressed. Thinking or hearing the words: fried, anger, bitter, apathy, confused, terror and despair, etc. are now designed to reset your or anyone's system.

The clouds dissipate once we catch the fear at work. We are no longer required to mindlessly go through the progression, pretending that we have no power. We choose. Be aware of what our words are activating.

Emotions are feelings that we have thought about. They are energized and they are powerful. They may appear to be a primary response yet they are secondary. This is the famous, "I think, I feel this way about it."

People around us in a state of fear/fiction, it can have an effect on the clouded mind. We choose it all therefore there is no such thing as contagion. The more subtle influences of our environment may begin to affect us through the higher layers of the auric field. When we are uneducated the fears of others can begin to make forgeries out of our thoughts.

Anything called illness is simply fear/guilt. Anything "malfunctioning," is doing so because that part of us is not being recognized as lovable. We create it all. Be able to love it all and we are always lovable.

Seeing oneself as an infinite creator, and remembering that we have created this entire situation, is the new vogue. Since everything is love, just understand this version of the love that you have authored for yourself and for the situation. This love is so powerful that it agreed to the dance with the fear within. Allow that universal sympathy to do its job. Repeat: I love to be me.

The Difference Between Fear and Information is Consciousness.

The difference between fear and information is the level of consciousness we hold. In anything that we came here to do there is a connection by which we recognize the boundaries of our project. These boundaries are almost always installed by fear, especially when we are children. Examples are: The Old Testament, Sinister minister, don't cross without looking both ways. Don't do that you might hurt yourself, stranger/danger etc.

It remains the small child's technique to explore the world boldly. As this person grows the idea is to allow them to police their own borders and continue the exploration unabashed. We accelerate when we trust and all other human beings to be in charge of themselves.

On worlds more advanced than ours, there are rights of passage that involve switching off fear and turning on awareness. These beings are reinitialized as adults in ceremony. There is homage to it on our planet. As we advance, so will these rituals.

Continuing with the theme of transmutation of concepts as related to understanding: The difference between an insult and constructive criticism is the level of consciousness we hold. The difference between a good experience and a bad experience is the level of understanding.

The "unhealed" urban scene is seen as love when acknowledged as a place where people have decided to experience evolution as adaptation. The bucolic life is easily recognizable as love where evolution is chosen in the form of flow. Flow and adaptation are identical twins. Remember whenever any information is presented to us as fear, it is automatically spurious.

All of these symptoms of fear vanish once we make the decision begin the reeducation and to recognize the opportunity that life is. As a rule people easily outgrow the fear of death. Ever ask yourself about the <u>fear of life</u>? Choose to celebrate life, in all its forms and especially yours.

Protocol Affirmation: Love is easy.

Protocol Nine

It' All Part of the Contract

This is one of the singularly most comforting protocols. "Be cool," is synonymous with this thought. Think it and instantaneously guilt vanishes. It is summary. As far as the release of anything that could be described as low self-esteem, it is panacea. It recreates anyone as a "Natural."

Another thing about this protocol is that it will increase one's relationship skills. We are always functioning in the way, that is as evolved as we can possibly be, at the particular time. At every moment we are living up to our contract, always, there are no exceptions. Lazy, stupid, late, failure and many more words are not real. Don't think with them any more.

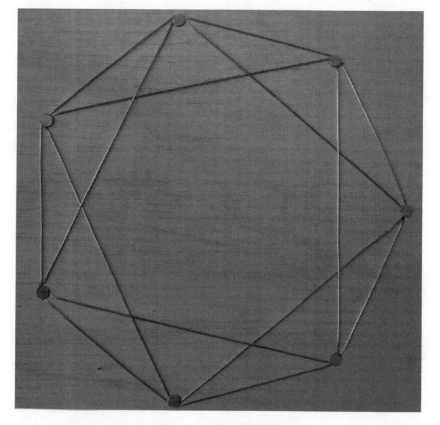

Seven sided Grid

Lets say we have just ended a two-week nicotine, caffeine, alcohol fast. Waking up hung over, we "forget," and light a cigarette while drinking a cup of coffee. Thus sucking the coffee up the cigarette like a straw. Well we have done this perfectly, functioning in the hundredth percentile.

Anyone else may regard us as slovenly, uncoordinated or perhaps comedically challenged, yet we have performed ideally as regarding our evolutionary mandate. That taste left in the mouth by that brew may have been the point at which we actually make the decision to change. Nothing less than this particular taste bud bludgeoning would have seen it through.

Everyone else is at the top of their game all times as well. No matter what the other person has done, or is doing, they are as evolved as they can be for the time slot they are in.

In knowing this fact we can give up a huge percent of judgmentalness about our fellow creature and therefore improve greatly our relationship quotient. When we are judgmental we are automatically less evolved than we could be. I forgive me, I love me. I forgive the other person, I love the other person.

Our incarnational contract has some even larger implications. When your author was in high school a thought appeared. This thought was in French and therefore conspicuous. To date no other foreign language had been studied. The translation amounted to, "Be in a state unchallenged by life." It had started upon a serious recognition of the existence of the opposite sex.

Many years later it became apparent that this nugget of philosophy had been inherited from a past life. It was part of the contract, just not the contract in this life. Since then many things have been designated to be passed on to my future selves. Shortly the question becomes, "What are you going to leave yourself for a future life time?"

Change

We all came here to grow and change. We have always had a love/fear relationship with change. Actually it turns out that there is only the one reason for this love/"hate" dichotomy. It frightens us because of our belief that change is unpredictable and has the potential to be for the "worse." We love it because of the potential of freedom it is. The one reason is potential.

The word potential is very sleep inducing. We frighten and stress our children by using it to describe them. "Oh, my child what great potential you have." We do away with common sense by delaying a satisfactory life because of the potential the future represents. All in all the self-empowerment protocol in this situation is: the renown being here now. Just keep saying, "I give myself permission to be here this instant."

"It's all part of the contract." The scope of this protocol is universal. Use it and be automatically in charge. The circuitous thinking normally distracting us doesn't even begin. It keeps us off the tilt. On top instantly, then one can deal with whatever is coming up. Re-set, new breath, failsafe, invite this ability into your life. Say it out loud a few times and you will be touted as a sage. And don't we all love that.

Protocol Affirmation: My understanding is always on hand.

Protocol Ten

<u>Activating A Protocol</u>

It is time to for a self-correction diagnostic whenever we feel badly. It's just a matter of noticing that we feel badly. It comes rather easily to us, both feeling badly and noticing. We are now adding the concept of triggering a protocol as the reaction to this observation/feeling.

That sinking feeling in the pit of the stomach is guilt. It's the physical body's signal to re-language something. That loss of life from the solar plexus goes away with the self-love discipline, "What ever it is, it will turn out to be the next step in my healing." Repeat this enough times and you'll live in a different and even "safer" world. There is nothing that happens that in not on your side.

When a thought just keeps repeating itself, it's a signal for a protocol. This would be the Dismissificator. Viewing things with compassion instead of ego, automatically catapults us up the spiral.

Wand

When a thought is made of guilt, we can view our action in it as having been perfect at the time of the event. Self-love is the basis of love of all things, because after all we are all one thing.

Confusion, lack of focus, is another signal. The decision-making faculty is temporarily off line. It means that guilt has taken over as our thinking. The short circuit may be due to the mitigation that is taking emotional responsibility for some one capable of taking care of themselves. It could also be self-blame. Blaming yourself is still blame. We are all functioning perfectly, no matter what we think it looks like. This specific protocol is in "Guilt Puppetry."

Sudden anger is another prompt. It means that something has crossed a border. Examine this boundary and when it is a valid one, calmly explain its presence as a personal preference.

As conclusion the point of this book is to get us each to self-correct. This is to say to become whole, to be our own authority and always our own councilor. To assist another we first become capable of assisting ourselves. We can all do this. It's just a matter of a little education or re-education. Remember, anything that makes a bad feeling indicates the opportunity to animate a protocol.

Affirmation Protocol: I integrate when I activate.

Protocol Eleven

<u>Qualifying for a License to Create Reality</u>

The first thing that we know when someone says that they will never reincarnate again is that they are going to reincarnate again. We know that they will be back because of the amount of resistance they are mounting. They have not yet gotten the bigger picture.

Any of us who have watched a stressed parent attending a child have commented to the effect that people ought to have a license to bring children into the world. You know, a written exam and a road test, just like a drivers license. We are not in their shoes and being judgmental always lowers the level of consciousness we are creating.

As we walk through this world, the way in which people act and create their life seems to be in the same category. We just find our selves in a set of circumstances. We may or may not know how we created it, and rarely know that we are sovereign of it.

The information contained with in these few pages is designed to keep us cognizant of the amount of power and authority we actually have. This book is like the Cliff Notes for Life. Each moment of our creation of life has a set of guidelines. Until we each recognize and understand them, things may not be all that they could be; yet life will continue to be fun. Remember, if it's not funny, it's not healed.

Waveform generator

Forgiving VS Loving

When I was on the other side, after having been shot to death, I met with the person, (being) who was the one that actually shot me. This meeting was far back in time and we were signing the contract for the event. He said, "Ya know I'm gonna blow your head off when you are twenty-seven years old." I said, "Ya, I know." Then we both laughed and laughed.

When I returned from the other side, I woke up in a hospital able to see people in their past lives. I still have this ability and it is joyous. I never found out what happened to my shooter. However I do know some things.

If you have ever met someone that has killed another person, and you ask them how they feel about it. Their eyes will go to the floor and they will say that they would give anything to have not have had it happen.

The person who shot me put themselves in this position while I was put into position to write this book, explore people's past lives for their benefit, create many television shows, works of art etc... I love this person for shooting me. I never forgave them because there was never anything to forgive. Forgive is a victim concept. Loving is a universal concept. Being shot to death? I love that person for doing it!

When we are at the point that we no longer are required to incarnate, then we will have mastered the love of the all. Personally I'm looking forward to my next incarnation. About ten years ago I decided that I would be male again.

Being Human (A New Model)

"Survival" has become an urban legend. Still we wrestle with it. No one in all histories did not survive. Reincarnation was doubtlessly involved. Truth, we are all endless. Each of us is an infinite fount of creation and creativity.

We have spent lifetimes bullied by guilt, drained by fictitious self-image and lessened by belief. Stop it, just stop it. The time has come for something new.

Love, imagination, choice, love, imagination, choice, ride it like a bicycle. Our world-reality is ours to create. Your reality is yours to create.

Protocol Affirmation: Clarity comes naturally to me.

Love You for No Reason,

R. Neville Johnston

A License to Create Reality

**May also be used as an Artistic License,
Poetic License or Creative License.**

- I recognize all things as love.
- I create 100% of my life AND I remember this all the time.
- I choose freewill over victim hood.
- I know that my thoughts are my life. There is no separation.
- I recognize everything in my life as my creation and I love it as though it were my child. Noting was ever done to me. It's all done by me. Therefore I am in charge of it.
- The Trinity of Human Power makes itself apparent in everything I do. I give myself permission to be who I really am.
- The Teflon Trinity is my way of life. I recognize my ability to delete guilt from my existence. Any conflict sets off a conscious diagnostic. This leads to the identification of any dysfunctional languaging codes and then goes immediately to the joy inherent in the event.
- I have converted my polar thinking into Trinity and am preparing to switch to quadrangulation.
- Any thought which cause me pain is a byproduct of primitive thinking. Any thought which brings me joy is an ascended thought.
- I am magnificent and I love being me!

Sign/date _____

Witness/date _____

Other Books by R. Neville Johnston

The Language Codes
Hidden Language Codes

The Language Codes and *Hidden Language Codes*, are easy to get:

We will use this analogy, if you had a computer with a defective program, that computer would take forever if it worked at all. In our human computer, and by this we mean our brain, in our human computer our name for a program is literally word. What I am saying is that if you have a word in your head you have a program running.

Lets take a look at the program "betrayal." What we humans are good at is recognizing. If you have the word betrayal in your head I can guarantee that you will recognize it. When we recognize betrayal, it sets of an extensive program that breaks down to various forms of hatred. First we hate the other person for being true to their own nature, that is duplicitous. We are all duplicitous, one decision at one time and another decision at another time. Secondly, we hate ourselves for not recognizing the now obvious signs that were right in front of us. And everyone hates us for not shutting up about it.

Fifteen years after the "betrayal" a little light goes ding and we realize that if that person had not done what they did we would probably still be with them and who knows what trash would be on the street about us by now. That event was not a betrayal, it was a blessing.

Do we stop using the word betrayal? No it invites us in another time, just like the Seiren's song and off we go again. It could be so different!

The books are lists of words that are latterly killing us, and how to change the programming that is creating all this. They are like Norton, a software package, a delete key, a fire wall. They are the upgrade we all know is out there, (actually in here.)

A word is a decision made. Many of these words are not making kind decisions for us. While it is true that information rides on the current of words that is our speech. It's the selection of these words that create the reality we live.

The difference between the two books is five years, teaching the subject many times. Different vocabulary is examined in each volume. Choose both.

Author contact information:

R. Neville Johnston

2210 Coppersmith Sq.

Reston VA. 20191

e-mail at telepathicguy@Yahoo.com

Website at www.telepathictv.com

Or call 703.860.2333

About the Author

In 1997 R. Neville Johnston was shot to death in a mugging in Manhattan. On the other side he was greeted by angels and began a new awareness. Aspects of his personal life were revealed to him. He was given many new abilities, new ways to think and new ways to be. Underscored is the awareness that, our beliefs create the reality in which we live.

This N.D.E. (Near Death Experience) or Shaman's Death was just the beginning. He chose to return, to assist we who are the human family, and to raise our consciousness.

Waking up in the hospital, able to see people in their past lives started the ball rolling. Since then he has been guiding people to a place where they can see their former incarnations for themselves. As well, future lives, off planet lives and parallel lives all seen through our own eyes.

At the same time he has written a series of books on just how powerful the words we think in are, in creating the reality we live in. Eleven Self Empowerment Protocols, is the next logical step. We all have with in us the ability to self-correct. This ability to a very large extent has been lost to us. Along with this went our ability to trust our own judgment. This volume will correct this and a lot more.

Bibliography

Barns, Coleman. *The Soul of Rumi*, San Francisco: Harper San Francisco, 2001.

Budge, Wallis E.A. *Egyptian Magic*, New York: Outlet Book Company Inc. 1991, Originally Published: K. Paul, Trench, Trubner, London, 1899.

Godwin, Joscelyn. *The Mystery of the Seven Vowels*, Grand Rapids, MI: Phanes Press, 1991.

Hauck, Dennis William. *The Emerald Tablet*, New York: Penguin Compass, 1999.

Jenkins, John Major. *Maya Cosmogenesis 2012*, Rochester VT: Bear & Co., 1998.

Kenyon, Tom & Essene, Virginia. *The Hathor Material*, Orcas, WA: ORB Communications, 1996.

Malchizedek, Drunvalo. *Ancient Secrets of the Flower of Life, Volume 1&2*, Flagstaff AZ: Light Technology Publishing, 1997.

Malchizedek, Drunvalo. *Living in the Heart*, Flagstaff AZ: Light Technology Publishing, 2003.

Malchizedek, Drunvalo. *Serpent of Light*, San Francisco CA: Weiser Books, 2007.

Redfield, James. *The Celestine Prophecy*, New York: Warner
Books,
1993.
Urantia Foundation. *The Urantia Book*, Chicago:
UrantiaFoundation, 1955.
Winters, Randolph. *The Pleiadian Mission*, Rancho Mirage
CA:
The Pleiades Project, 1994.
Yogananda, Paramahansa. *Autobiography of a Yogi*, Nevada
City
CA: Crystal Clarity Publishers, 1946.

Manufactured By: RR Donnelley
Breinigsville, PA USA
January, 2011